Mastering
Web 2.0

Mastering Web 2.0

Transform your business using
key website and social media tools

Susan Rice Lincoln

KOGAN PAGE

London and Philadelphia

First published in Great Britain and the United States in 2009 by Kogan Page Limited

120 Pentonville Road
London N1 9JN
United Kingdom
www.koganpage.com

525 South 4th Street, #241
Philadelphia PA 19147
USA

© Susan Rice Lincoln, 2009

ISBN 978 0 7494 5466 1

British Library Cataloguing-in-Publication Data

A CIP record for this book is available from the British Library.

Library of Congress Cataloging-in-Publication Data

Lincoln, Susan Rice.
   Mastering Web 2.0 : transform your business using key website and social media tools / Susan Rice Lincoln
      p. cm.
   ISBN 978-0-7494-5466-1
   1. Internet marketing. 2. Viral marketing. 3. Web 2.0. 4. Electronic commerce
—Social aspects. I. Title.
   HF5415.1265.L57 2009
   658.8′72--dc22
                                                    2008053903

Typeset by Saxon Graphics Ltd, Derby
Printed and bound in India by Replika Press Pvt Ltd

To Chloe and Gabriella:
your energy, your laughter and your love are forever an inspiration

And for my mother:
the world is less bright without you

Contents

Preface

Making sense of Web 2.0: Weaving the confusing fragments into a strategic whole

When this book comes out, it will be 2009. Google will have just turned 10. Amazon is a blockbuster site. YouTube is a phenomenon. Facebook is the favourite daily companion of thousands of people.

But for the handful of success stories out there, there are millions and millions of companies, websites and internet experiments that are floundering in cyberspace – ineffectual, dormant or spinning around in utter confusion.

Why? Why is it that so few have really been able to successfully capture the power of the internet? *Why have so many individuals and companies been unable to make sense of it all?*

The answer is that most of us lack a strong strategic sense of where we want to go. We are confused by the myriad of options. We grasp at straws. We scramble around trying to make sense of fragments – tactics, tools, random ideas – rather than grasping the big picture. We desperately need to understand how our companies and our products can communicate effectively, cohesively and holistically.

But for the moment we are stuck with the fragments.

Our media world is in fragments. Many of our offline media choices don't work as well as they used to. As for our online choices, we are unclear which ones to use or if any of them really work. Many internet tools are seductive but we don't really 'get' how they can add to our bottom line. As consumers exert more control over the information they listen to and create, we aren't totally sure where we fit in.

Our audience is also in fragments. They are all over the place. For starters, our consumers are much more splintered in their viewing habits than ever before. But even more importantly, consumers – ie everyone – are fragmented in their attention. Attention scarcity is the new buzzword of the 21st century. Almost everyone today is drowning, awash with information overload. We all take in much more than we are capable of digesting. The sheer volume of stimuli has us all struggling. So it is hardly surprising that it is more and more difficult to get our messages heard above the din.

Because our budgets are tighter, we can't be everywhere at once. So instead we are nowhere.

Probably most dangerous is that our overall understanding of what is happening around us is also in fragments. We may *think* we understand the internet and the newer Web 2.0 tools. But we read about these things in bits and pieces: an article about social networking here, a comment about the strengths of blogs there. Interesting ideas. Captivating thoughts. But it is difficult to get a broad perspective on the social media terrain. Almost impossible to grasp our communications options in a solid, simple, streamlined way.

I wrote this book to bring the fragments together. I wrote this book so that you – as an individual entrepreneur or a large company – can use the internet not just as a technological tactical tool but as a strategic communication powerhouse which will drive your sales and your customer relationships to new heights. I wrote this book because I did not believe that the simple, straightforward story of the internet today had been told – or told well.

At the end of the book I provide you with a strategic tool – the Web Wheel – which will help you begin to understand how you can put the pieces of the puzzle together. The Web Wheel is there to help you make informed decisions. To create intelligent, strategic and holistic choices for your marketing programme.

There is an additional, final point I would like to emphasize. We are all in love with technology and what it offers us. But after gorging myself on infinite blogs, websites, social networking sites, viral marketing campaigns and podcasts, a very important thought dawned on me.

In our giddiness about technology, we have forgotten one very important point. At the end of the day it is not the technology that is important. *What is important is what that technology allows us to do – which is to communicate better. The better we communicate to our consumer, the more we can ultimately sell. And selling more to the right target audience is the ultimate point we are trying to reach.*

Communications and selling are the key words. Not technology.

This book therefore is about the changing world of communication. As a company – even if you are only an individual – you compete against endless other companies in your daily quest to stand out. Over their deafening cries, you must make an invincible mark on the world in which you live and compete.

Keep a clear eye on the goal, which is not to master 'tools' but to communicate better and in a more authentic way.

Lift your head above the fray.

And you will find your clear, unique and convincing voice in the din.

The potential – *your* potential – is immense.

Strip the fragments away.

Embrace what the internet can do for you today and into the future.

Introduction

Pearl-like possibilities in an old/new world: Managing your options as you create your web strategy

> We're still in the first minutes of the first day of the internet revolution.
>
> Scott Cook, Chairman of Intuit, Inc, 2000 (reported by Steven Levingston, *International Herald Tribune*)

A power that boggles the mind

Possibilities.

Simple, glorious, pearl-like possibilities.

Nothing shouts possibilities more than the internet. Nothing has transformed our lives more than the internet. It ranks right up there with the automobile, the printing press and the telephone.

The internet allows us to do anything; we are limited only by our imagination. We can talk. Argue. Express our opinions. Create. Make new friends. Connect with old ones. Participate in politics. Inspire. Get inspired. Sell products, services, ideas. Establish our reputations. Or destroy them.

The internet's power boggles the mind.

Figure 0.1   Tap into the power of today's internet revolution

Getting your arms around the internet is like hugging a grizzly bear

Putting your arms around the internet is a bit like hugging a grizzly bear. You gape at the beauty, the power, the sheer irresistibility of the thing. But no matter how seductive, a grizzly is a very frightening thing. And many of us – particularly companies – poke at the internet today with great trepidation.

The only way to hug the internet grizzly bear is to understand it and handle it carefully with forethought and strategic finesse.

It is for this reason that I have written this book. To help all of us – from small individuals to the biggest companies – understand. To strip away the hype, to clear away the smoke and fully grasp the powerful possibilities the internet has in store for us. To outline the pros and cons of all the basic internet tools available today.

This book is not for techies or utopian visionaries; it is for the rest of us

In my research I noticed there are roughly three types of information about the internet.

First, there are reams of how-to books: technological treatises about how to create a podcast or a video or a blog. At the other end of the spectrum are what I call the utopian books. Books that wax eloquent about how the newest kid on the block – social media – can transform all of our lives. How we are at the precipice of a new industrial revolution.

Finally, there is an unbelievably confusing array of information on the internet itself. There is too much information, much of it written poorly and often overly technical.

But what about information for the rest of us? If you are not a techie, the how-to books are probably too detailed and technical to shed light on your issues. If you are a busy employee, manager or CEO, you don't have the time to swim through a baffling amount of information on the internet. As for the 'visionaries', their picture of the world is seductive, but most of us live in what I call the old/new world. We may be tempted by utopian dreams but we still live in a world of conservative, controlling hierarchies and risk-averse companies. We want to understand how the internet and its tools fit into the real – not a dream – world.

Where are you on the internet journey?

Marketing to the social web is a journey, not a destination.

Weber, 2007

We are all in different places in our internet journey. Some of us still struggle with our basic websites, others have been swept away by social media fever, and most of us – for lack of a better word – are rather confused.

Wherever you are, it is my hope that this book will speak to you. The bulk of this book is a kaleidoscope tour around some of today's internet's most famous characters: blogs, social networking sites, podcasts, search engine optimization, article marketing, websites, video casts, viral marketing. Depending on where you are on your journey, you will find yourself somewhere on the instructional continuum. Each chapter will surprise with highly fresh material or will serve as an in-depth review, pulling together the bits and pieces with which you were already familiar.

An important note is that while this book covers a lot of ground, by necessity it does not include every single topic imaginable. The choice of what to include remains always somewhat arbitrary. But the hope is that the topics covered in this book form a complete communications package, a full menu from which you can choose as you converse with prospects, customers, employees or suppliers. Coupled with a clear strategy, the ensemble will give you a unique and modern voice.

This book was written from a specific vantage point

Admittedly, this book has been written from a very specific vantage point.

I am a layperson, not a techie. I write web copy, so I can navigate easily around the web. But at the core, I am a communication expert more than an internet aficionado, As a consultant, I have developed countless communication strategies for companies ranging from Nike to Ericsson, LEGO to Wrangler. I view most issues as an internationalist. I am an American who has lived in Europe for over 25 years and have worked on dozens of global projects. And, finally, I am a pragmatist. I firmly believe that the internet is the most exciting event in most of our lives. But I do not believe that it offers us utopia.

The Wild West

When it comes to the internet, we will always straddle two worlds: the 'real' world of political and hierarchical constraints, and the world of internet dreams. The challenge is not to dream about one and bemoan the other. The idea is to understand that these two worlds coexist. We can create better, exciting solutions using internet tools. But there will often be walls obstructing our path – corporate hurdles as well as personal prejudice. The goal is to work through these blocks and create constructive solutions in a less than ideal world.

Many have likened the internet of today to the Wild West. But the Wild West was not utopia. Like the internet today, it was a place where there were new rules and new tools and people were learning on the hoof. But even those setting out new frontiers had old roots and old mentalities and traditional ways of thinking. Just like the internet today.

1 Social media – giving power to the people

New media which changes the communications game forever

> Our mind's desire is to know and to understand. Our heart's desire is to be known and to be understood. When I have been listened to and when I have been heard, I am able to re-perceive my world in a new way and go on.
>
> Carl Rogers, 1964

Let's start by clarifying some terms.

The internet today has many names. Web 2.0 is one. Social media is another.

Web 2.0: defining the indefinable

Web 2.0 is an unclear term. Ask 100 technology people to define Web 2.0 and you will most likely get 100 different answers (blog posting, 2007, by Lani and Allen Volvod).

The term was originally created by Tim O'Reilly of O'Reilly Media. He described Web 2.0 as 'the business revolution in the computer industry'(Wikipedia).

According to Stephen Fry, a technology writer for *The Guardian*, Web 2.0 is an idea in people's heads more than anything else. For Fry, this idea is all about interaction, participation and reciprocity. In a web 2.0 world, people can upload as easily as they can download (Wikipedia).

The difference between Web 2.0 and Web 1.0

Bart Decrem, a founder and former CEO of 'Flock (web browser)', calls web 2.0 the 'participatory web' and regards the web-as-information-source as web 1.0 (Wikipedia).

Web 1.0 is static and is more of a place to find information than a forum for sharing ideas or creating new products together.

Web 2.0 is a web in which people can interact and participate rather than just read. A good way to picture web 2.0 is as the world's biggest café, whereas the earlier web was the world's biggest library.

A web 1.0 world is a world of simple transactions. A web 2.0 world is a model where you to go a blog, see what people are saying, leave a comment, check out links to other sites, leave a comment, compare user experiences, buy something, comment on the experience and then leave.

Web 2.0 is messier. It is warmer. It is more human.

Table 1.1 summarizes the differences between the two. As we go through the book, many of these differences should become clearer.

Social media is more about behaviour than a set of tools

> Taking an active role in creating a dialogue with customers about issues that they care about, at the moment in time when they care about those concerns, is the heart of social media marketing.
>
> Solis and Livingston, 2007

Because of the ambiguity of the term Web 2.0, many people prefer to use the term social media.

Table 1.1 Highlighting the differences between Web 1.0 and Web 2.0

	Web 1.0	**Web 2.0**
Mode	Read	Write and Contribute
Primary unit of content	Page	Post/record
State	Static	Dynamic
Viewed through...	Web browser anything	Browsers, RSS reader
Architecture	Client server	Web services
Content created by...	Web coders	Everyone
Domain of...	Geeks	Mass amatuerization

Source: Universal McCann

Wikipedia defines social media as 'all online tools and platforms that people use to share opinions, insights, experiences and perspectives with each other'. The social web is a place where people with common interests gather to share thoughts and comments. Importantly, social media holds increasing sway over public opinion.

Many people define social media by their tools (blogging, Twitter, social networking, wikis, RSS, photo sharing, video sharing, podcasting, widgets, chat rooms, message boards – see Figure 1.1).

Figure 1.1 Summary of key social media tools

But social media is more a behaviour than a set of tools. In other words, social media is more about the ideas that you share, collaborate on, create and participate in rather than observe:

- Social media embraces the 'architecture of participation' (Wikipedia). In other words, users can actually add value to the applications they use.

- Social media captures collective intelligence. Through them, we can work seamlessly together in teams, no matter how geographically dispersed.

- Social media is accessible, easy to use and understand. There are low barriers to entry. Social media tools are both versatile and flexible.

- Social media makes it easy for us to share information with small niches. Picking up from Chris Anderson's famous article and book, *The Long Tail*, social media help us to touch the smallest of markets, the most niche of interests.

- With social media, an individual can shift easily between the role of audience and the role of author. With easy-to-use software, ordinary individuals can create their own content and seamlessly share it with others.

An example of social media is Wikipedia, an online encyclopedia. This is an encyclopedia like no other. Entries can be added by any web user... and edited by any other. An extreme experiment in trust, it works extremely well, An example of a new dynamic in individual content creation, Wikipedia ranks in the top 100 websites.

Social media gives people power

User-generated media is at the heart of social media. With a snap of a finger, ordinary citizens are transformed into citizen journalists – writers, radio broadcasters and film makers. Ordinary people have power like they never have had before.

And inherent in that ability are the seeds of a revolution. Social media gives a potential power to ordinary people that they have never enjoyed before in the history of mankind.

Most people were confined to relatively limited economic rules, whether as passive consumers of mass-produced products or employees trapped deep within organizational bureaucracies where the boss told them what to do. Even their elected representatives barely concealed their contempt for bottom-up participation in decision making. In all, too many people were bypassed in the circulation of knowledge, power and capital, and thus participated at the economy's margins.

Today the tables are turning. The growing accessibility of information technologies puts the tools required to collaborate, create value and compete at everybody's fingertips. This liberates people to participate in innovation and wealth creation within every sector of the economy.

Tapscott and Williams, 2008

The most exciting part of the new web is the change in mindset and philosophy. This is a world in which the audience – ie all of us, rather than an elite – decides what is important.

What's all the fuss about?

What's all the racket about? We hear so much about blogs and social networking sites. What is the big deal?

The best way to illustrate the importance of Web 2.0 or the new social media is by looking at some simple tables. The first two show the results from a Universal McCann global study of active internet users and their experience of / exposure to various forms of new media. The results are simply astonishing; this isn't a groundswell, but a veritable stampede (see Tables 1.2 and 1.3).

Despite its wild popularity with individuals, Web 2.0 is still in its early days for corporations. The following few charts show by industry and region how Web 2.0 is being used. Not surprisingly, the most developed industry is technology. But with the exception of instant messaging, Web 2.0 has not really taken off in any sector.

There are many reasons for this reticence. Part of it is lack of knowledge and confusion about how to handle the internet. Part of it is that the new media require a new mindset which is diametrically opposed to the the closed, controlling, top-down model of most

Table 1.2   How people use social media around the world

Read blog	72.5%
Read personal blogs	67.5%
Visit a photosharing website	63.2%
Manage a profile on an existing social network	57.3%
Leave a comment on a blog	54.8%
Upload my photos	52.2%
Leave a comment – news site	45.8%
Download a podcast	45.1%
Start my own blog	38.7%
Upload a video	38.5%
Subscribe to an RSS feed	33.7%

Source: Universal McCann

Table 1.3   Numbers of people using social media around the world

	%
Watch video clips online	82.9
Read blog	72.5
Read personal blogs	67.5
Visit a photo sharing website	63.2
Manage a profile on an existing social network	57.3
Leave a comment on a blog	54.8
Upload my photos	52.2
Leave a comment–news site	45.8
Download a podcast	45.1
Start my own blog	38.7
Upload a video	38.5
Subscribe to an RSS feed	33.7

Source: Universal McCann

companies. Also, most companies have not figured out how to fully monetize the millions of people who flock to social networking sites like MySpace, Facebook and YouTube. Finally, many businesses are not convinced that the time and energy that many social media tools take are really worthwhile. They are not clear about the ROI, so they steer clear of it altogether.

But social media is here to stay and are changing – and will change the rules of the game. The companies who establish themselves in Web 2.0 tools will be well ahead of the game, positioning themselves as leaders in their field (see Figures 1.2, 1.3 and 1.4).

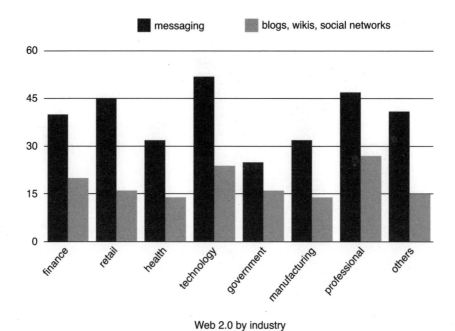

Web 2.0 by industry

Figure 1.2 How different industries use Web 2.0

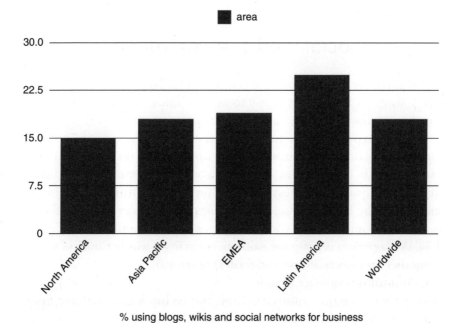

% using blogs, wikis and social networks for business

Figure 1.3 How social media are used in companies around the world

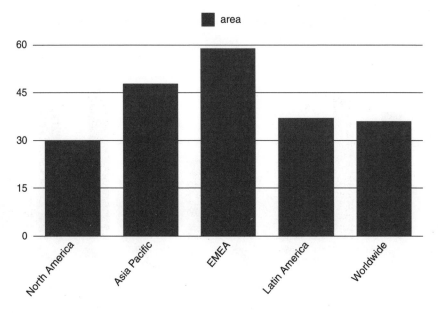

% using instant or text messaging for business

Figure 1.4   How companies around the world use instant/text messaging

Social media = community

Social media is synonymous with community. People want to connect. They want to talk. They want to share. They belong to whatever community they want – no matter how big or small.

It is no surprise that communities that focus on a specific common interest are one of the fastest growing applications on the web. There are hundreds of examples. IToolbox.com is a community for information technology professionals. They share opinions and information on the latest technology products and services. BootsnAll.com is a place where budget travellers share advice about hotels (Figure 1.5). iVillage.com is a site for women, covering a whole range of topics from diet and sex to home and food (Figure 1.6).

Communities validate people.

It is therefore the cultures behind the technologies that are fascinating, not the technologies themselves.

Figure 1.5 BootsnAll Travel – a community of budget travellers

Figure 1.6 iVillage – a community site for women

As Microsoft CEO Steven A Ballmer told the *New York Times* in a discussion about the future of software:

> I think one pervasive change is the increasing importance of community. That will come in different forms, with different age groups of people, and it will change as the technology evolves. But the notion of multiple people interacting on things – that will forever continue. That's different today, and we're going to see those differences build. You see it in a variety of ways now, in social networking sites, in the way people collaborate at work, and in ad hoc collaboration over the internet... It's a big deal.
>
> Quoted in Weber, 2007

The conclusion? *The killer application of the web is people.*

In a profound sense, the internet today is no different from what it has always been: a place for humans to connect and transcend time, place and language.

The internet is all about humanity. And the important fact about social media is that it lets humans be more human than ever before.

2 Communicating the best and the worst

Making sure that your web strategy says something worthwhile

> Once you express yourself you can tell the world what you want from it or how you would like to change it.
>
> Jacqueline Kennedy Onassis

To my mind, the internet is a communications vehicle with no equal. And the new net – complete with social media tools – is evolving the potential to communicate at breakneck speed. The possibilities of exchange and sharing, participation and content creation can make your head swim.

But as with all things in life, there are always two sides to every coin. And it is safe to say that social media is the best and worst thing that could have ever happened to communications.

Let's start with the bad news.

The communication paradox

One of the great paradoxes of today's world is that while we are able to communicate like never before, the quality of communications is abysmal. We are dying of hunger while being simultaneously surrounded by an embarrassment of riches.

Despite instant messaging and e-mails and Twitter and Facebook and the blogosphere, we may very well be communicating less well than ever before. *Put another way, there's a lot of 'stuff' out there, but is it really good communication?*

A little case in point: on my Twitter account, I am constantly being notified of people's every movement. 'We are eating pancakes', 'We are swimming at the lake now', 'I slept badly last night.'

Do I care?

Is this where the 'social media revolution' leads us?

Aside from some of the perturbing philosophical questions it poses (are people living their lives or simply chronicling them?), the real question is:

Is any of this good communications?

Exciting tools don't necessarily translate into exciting communications

I have advised hundreds of clients about good communications. To my mind, any communication worth its salt must be clear, focused, tight and specific: all of the things that social media – with their meandering, wandering stream-of-consciousness manner – are not.

Yes, social media offers us a *different type* of communication.

Yes, social media gives us a *lot* of communication (much of it unwelcome).

But is it *good*? Does it go to the point? Does it leave the viewer or participant with a new sense of understanding? Or is it just muddle?

The answer, of course, is somewhere in the middle. Some is good, some is okay; and some is shockingly bad.

But the frightening thing is that no one seems to care. Social media proponents have no time for what they call corporate 'gobbledegook'. Yet they are busy making a lot of gobbledegook of their own.

Vomiting all and any thoughts, no matter how irrelevant, the rule of the day is the more, the merrier. Who cares about communicating? Who cares about *saying* something? Let's just talk and talk and talk. And the recipient gets buried under the junk or gives up in despair.

One thing is for sure: exciting social media tools don't necessarily translate into exciting communications.

Communication just for communication's sake doesn't move the boat forward. Good communication takes discipline, thought and not a little pencil-biting. It isn't endless stream-of-consciousness or the jotting down of random, disjointed thought, which is so prevalent nowadays on the new net.

Social media is infinite

One of the reasons why social media doesn't always deliver consistently stellar communications is hardwired in its DNA. By its very nature, social media is infinite. There are lots of beginnings but far fewer endings. Conversations start out with a bang but trail off into a never-ending path of comments, links, new sites, new comments and new blogs.

You can literally spend days answering a query only to emerge with fifteen additional questions and – woefully – no answers. It's like going on a roller-coaster ride as you follow the ups and downs, twists and turns of various thoughts. Ideas float. Nothing is linear.

In the end, you end up more confused than you began.

Good communication is not a lot of words. Good communication says something.

I may be old-fashioned, but 'good' solid communication is worth its weight in gold. It does not meander. It does not get lost in a deafening cacophony of voices. It is considerate and thoughtful and has a purpose and *says something*. People who hear it walk away with new knowledge and deeper insights.

You can have all the qualities that social media offers – democratic, open, sharing, participative – and still not achieve good communication. Solid communication requires discipline and vision and forethought: qualities many people are frankly just too lazy to develop, as they scribble busily away on blogs, forums, wikis and various social networking sites. It's a pity, because this issue is far and away the Achilles heel of social media, and at some point will need to be addressed or the 'social media revolution' will descend into a bunch of inconsequential garble.

So this was the bad news. What about the good news?

Moving from mass media to me media

Gone are the paternalistic days of Citizen Kane – enter the days of the citizen journalist.

We were all bottle-fed on mass media – one ad message pushed out to one mass audience in the hope of seducing at least some of its members into buying the product. Mass media is built on efficiency – one message, one campaign, one audience.

Most of us are less familiar with consumer media, the core of web 2.0. Consumer media is me-oriented. User-generated content. Citizen journalists. Through blogs, podcasts and videos, people are now writers, radio broadcasters and film makers. Every single one of us is a potential media creator.

Our world will never be the same again.

Citizen journalism has caught the imagination of millions. Consumers want to be listened to rather than be listeners. They no longer want to respond to companies and their messages. They want companies to respond to them and their individual, niche needs.

The fact that citizen journalists create content in droves has changed something else: people don't look up as much to traditional media. There are alternatives to getting information from the big boys. A rampant lack of trust of professional media exists in part because we now can choose to go elsewhere, in part because of long years of abuse:

> We have seen fewer and fewer organizations able to continue to hold the public's trust as trust shifts to the peer space. The reason trust is shifting is because the original sources of information, business, mainstream media and government have egregiously violated that trust on a number of occasions in the past several years.
>
> Solis and Livingston, 2007

Furthermore, the growing trend in preferring consumer-generated media over professional media is not just about whether you will read the *New York Times* or get your news from your next-door neighbour's blog. It will also play a crucial role in how consumers will make their purchasing decisions. A recent report revealed that a whopping 71 per cent of consumers are more influenced by user-generated content when making a purchasing decision than by information generated by brand advertisers and marketers (Dan Morrison in article on iMediaConnection.com).

You control nothing

The new consumer-dominated media world upsets the proverbial applecart. In this world, everyone has access. Everyone can create content. Everyone can distribute. Everyone can participate. Everyone has an opinion – and that opinion holds weight.

In the old world of mass media you as advertiser or marketer controlled your message – both content and distribution. In the new world you control nothing (Figure 2.1).

Social media has the professional guys running scared. No longer are radio broadcasts, newspapers and television stations or public relations departments the domain of the professional elite. News belongs to all of us.

Ordinary citizens no longer need to be helpless, impotent observers. They can comment on issues, bolster (or destroy) products and form public opinion if they get in front of a large enough audience.

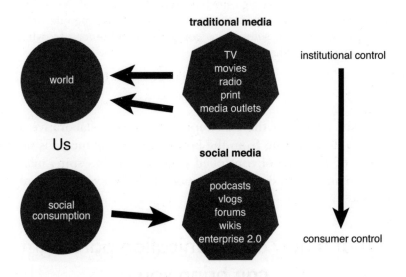

Figure 2.1 Social media turns the traditional rules of control upside down

Social media will turn communication on its head

Given its power, social media is therefore not just a new tool. It's much, much more. By letting any individual participate, it has changed forever how messages are created. Social media shifts the balance of power; message creation has been lifted out of the hands of a tiny elite and is now in the hands of all of us. And this is big, big news. This is the best thing that has happened to communication and all of us in a very, very long time.

Social media changes the rules. And what's more important is that one day soon, social media will be the only game in town.

Once upon a time, the professional elites (major media outlets as well as companies) created controlled communications, using top-down thinking and one-way monologue. Their world was a world of isolated competing fiefdoms either on- or offline. As a company, this was your world too. As Shel Holtz, co-podcaster and author of The Hobson and Holz Report podcast, says:

> Most marketers for a long time have had the luxury of delivering a message one way, top down, and they knew that people were going to listen, and some were going to be influenced by what they saw or what they heard.
>
> Quoted in Solis and Livingston, 2007

Social media stands for the exact opposite: open, collaborative, non-hierarchical and coming from the bottom up. Social media is utterly intolerant of any type of controlled communication: 'spin', manipulation or manufactured communication. It is, in every sense of the word, *real*.

What a new communication paradigm can bring you

If you are running a corporation, you must be wondering why on earth I think all of this is positive? What does social media bring you –

except bigger headaches? Why shouldn't you just throw your hands in the air in despair now that you have 'lost control'?

The fact is, the end of controlled manipulation is good for everyone. It means we can all breathe easier. We can all begin to work and behave in a more open manner, which is what our consumers have wanted all along.

But just because your consumers have more of a voice does not mean that you are silenced. You still have a say. An important one. The social media dynamic is not a zero-sum game. The pie is simply growing larger.

More than ever, you need to understand your message. You must hold steadfast to your vision. You must *have* a vision. You just can't push it on to people like you once may have done. You need to listen and craft your vision so that it is enriched by your consumer.

Yes, this is good news. It means your communication will be better, richer and more on target than they have ever been before.

Your messages will be better than ever

The shifting sands of change do not mean you have lost your foothold. They simply mean that as you create your vision and craft your message, you must first listen. Gather and digest ideas and comments your consumer base has to offer. Incorporate their intuitions into your thinking.

This is not a hardship duty. Consumers are full of rich intuitions about the products and services they buy. Consumers are not the enemy or laboratory rats to be kept at arm's length. They are your greatest ally and will help you to go from good to great.

3 Piggies in the middle

Successfully using new internet tools while working in an old-fashioned, conservative business world

A recent report covering 17 countries revealed that 16 per cent of the information workforce is 'hyperconnected', while an astonishing 50 per cent is 'passive', see Figure 3.1 (Steve Rubel in article on MicroPersuasion.com).

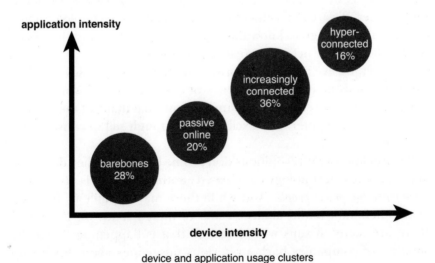

device and application usage clusters

Figure 3.1   The hyperconnected lead but many trail behind

These surprising numbers are confirmed in *Groundswell* by Charlene Li and Josh Bernoff, in which they estimate that 52 per cent of the US online population is passive.

Those who are fully engaged are way out ahead of the rest of us. This hyperconnected group are interesting, intelligent people caught up in the excitement of social media mania. They Twitter, they blog, they social network, they comment and link and podcast and videocast. Involved 24/7, they savour all that is the new net. They are evangelists.

The problem is that this group of hyperconnected people tend to be the spokespeople for what is happening on the internet today. And despite all their enthusiasm and knowledge, it is unclear if they fully understand where many of us are situated – dazed by the speed of change, confused by the fragmentation of media, uncertain how to move forward, and working for companies that cling dearly to old models.

They're talking about a revolution

The hyperconnected talk about revolution. They proclaim that the world will never be the same. And the workplace as we know it is in tatters.

What about the rest of us? Well, we may not be hyperconnected. In the course of our work, though, we probably know a fair amount about the internet. We are not techies but lead a somewhat technological life. We are savvy enough to know that things are changing and that social media and the new net offer great opportunities.

However, we live in the real world, with demanding bosses and time pressures and the constant presence of corporate profit worries and hard-to-please shareholders. We understand that many of these social media tools, no matter how exciting, are a tough sell in conservative environments.

We also know that revolutions don't come by magic. They don't just appear because technology has created another set of tools. *Revolutions come from one place: people.* And while there may be millions fired up about their new-found ability to talk to their friends on Facebook, there are many in suits who dread all that is happening. Even the smallest of companies harbour serious misgivings about giving up control; they worry about the consequences of being too open and sharing. They don't like to give up the family secrets and certainly do not want to risk the possibility that someone outside might see their imperfections.

The hyperconnected may not want to accept it, but the rest of us know that the social media revolution is in trouble. Ordinary people may be flocking to MySpace in droves, but there are just as many people sitting around boardrooms that are dampening its fires. With change comes fear. The old and new worlds are quietly drawing their battle lines.

The hyperconnected sometimes look down on us

It's not really their fault. But often the hyperconnected look down on us, disparage us. Read the blogs and you will feel the insidious sense of superiority. They nickname us the marketing dinosaurs. Or they criticize us for being too reticent to try new things. For the hyperconnected, we are simply too slow to get on the bandwagon of social media mania.

But these haughty hyperconnected attitudes are unfair (and, I might add, against the open spirit of social media in the first place). The rest of us are not stupid or slow. We just understand that sometimes it takes time to integrate new tools into an old environment. We might share the dreams of the hyperconnected. But we have a reality to deal with and it's looking over our shoulders.

The reality is that the revolution isn't here. Not yet.

New media has by no means replaced more traditional forms of communication. Television, for example, is far from being dead. So is TV advertising. It may not be a growth industry, but news of its death are greatly exaggerated.

Old coexists with the new. And it will continue to do so for the foreseeable future.

Ignoring the old doesn't make sense – forgetting about the new is foolhardy.

We end up being piggies in the middle

The result? Millions of us who work in companies of all sizes are piggies in the middle. We are trussed up, torn between the old and the new, and just trying to make things work. We want to move forward, we want to use the potential of the new net, but we aren't always sure how to do that as we face obstacles from old-fashioned thinking and top-down corporate structures.

Yes, we vaguely like the social media concepts. Yes, they seduce us. But as piggies in the middle, we remain loyal to a more traditional way of thinking about things. We try – without success – to reconcile the conservative world of business with the more modern, open sharing world that Web 2.0 represents. But we are blocked because companies to a greater or less extent have been built on 20th century corporate principles rather than 21st century technological breakthroughs which put the accent on ordinary people.

The roadblock for Web 2.0 is not the technology but the people who use the technology. CEOs who don't want to lose control. Marketing directors who view social media as just one more tool on a very long list. Bosses who can't tell the difference between a blog and a podcast – and aren't interested in learning more. None of these people are 'bad'. They are used to doing things a certain way. They resist change. They don't understand how in the long run social media will help a company's fundamentals. They cling desperately to control. They are, for lack of a better word, human beings.

And ultimately we know that as piggies in the middle our only friend will be time.

We will never catch up with the technology

The other day I was speaking to a good friend of mine in California who sneered that 'Web 2.0 is old news.' And somewhere it probably *is* old news. Therein lies the great irony of the eternal technological chase: just when the rest of us get used to the idea of using Web 2.0, the hyperconnected will have moved far ahead of us again to another tool, another subject, another revolution.

We will, quite simply, never catch up. We will always be running on empty. We will always be behind.

This is the frustration of infinite technology that grows in leaps and bounds – much faster than the people and companies who use the tools.

The tiny sliver of the population who are 'fully engaged' are not large in number. But we are left behind in the dust as these techno-bunnies hop headlong into the future.

Social media? If the truth be told, the vast majority of us are still struggling with our websites. Or search engine optimization on a good day. We do not live or work in an open, loose, uncontrolled and ultimately anti-corporate environment for which the hyperconnected clamour.

It's just not going to happen. Or at least not tomorrow.

We are squished between the old and the new. We are in the middle. Trapped between new media and traditional media. A new way of doing things and an old way of thinking. Consumers who want more – a new way – and companies who want to continue trudging away in tradition. We are in between the fleet-footed, switched-on techies and the digital Neanderthals. We seek workable solutions that make sense to disapproving bosses or skittish shareholders.

Piggies in the middle? We are trying to win at the game. We try to catch the ball. But we just don't quite know how to do it.

We are stuck.

It is my hope that this book will help you – and those around you – get a little unstuck. Help you understand what the web and its possibilities represent today. And how to strategically pick the tools that are right for you.

4 The making of the corporation/person

How companies can transform themselves by learning how to talk and think like a human being

Marketers of all sorts are now being urged to give up the steering wheel to a new breed of consumers who want more control over the ways products are peddled to them.

Weber, 2007

The power is with the consumer. Marketers and retailers are scrambling to keep up with her.

Stuart Elliot at the 96th Annual Conference of the Association of National Advertisers, quoted in Weber, 2007

Web 2.0 has great benefits for companies.

A G Lafley, Chief Executive of Procter & Gamble, quoted in Weber, 2007

For a company of any size, Web 2.0 carries many advantages, such as the ability to:

- generate leads;
- enhance search engine optimization;
- improve customer relationships;
- stay connected with business partners;
- conduct research and development;
- educate customers about new products;
- hear unfiltered voices/opinions of customers;
- provide opportunities for employees to talk directly to customers;
- provide customer service and support;
- communicate with your employees;
- position yourself as an industry thought leader.

But we still feel uncomfortable

Despite all the benefits, corporations still feel highly uncomfortable with social media in whatever form.

For a corporation, social media is scary. Really, really scary. Mainly because they can see the writing on the wall.

Web 2.0 is synonymous with change. Web 2.0 embraces a modern way of thinking and, to be used properly, requires corporations to alter their structures as well as their mindsets. Instead of operating as hierarchies with controlled communication, companies will need to endorse a new more open, sharing and collaborative relationship with their employees, partners and consumers.

As inevitable as it is, change is difficult.

Undoubtedly, there will be those who would like to dig themselves a deep hole, burying their heads in the sand to forget about the whole nasty business.

But even those dug deep in the sand will eventually begin to wonder and worry that they are missing out on something big.

The internet – and particularly social media – has that effect.

Who will help us get out of this mess?

A lot of businesses around the world wonder who is going to get them out of this mess. Who will lead them along a clear path to deal with the monumental changes as social media begins to force their hand? Will it be advertising agencies? (Despite their heavily laden, public relations driven promises to the contrary, they appear to be as clueless as everyone else.) Or social media agencies? (They seem to be making it up as they go along.)

Where is the answer? Who *can* help?

The answer lies in businesses finding their very humanity.

Enter the corporation as person

For decades I have worked as an international brand/communication specialist. My clients hail from the four corners of the globe and include household names like Gillette, Nike and LEGO.

I built my business on a very simple principle: consumers dream about their lives – they have hopes and deep-seated values to which they aspire; in turn, your company should have a vision, a set of values it stands for.

The key is to identify and understand the place where your consumer's dream intersects with your company's dream (Figure 4.1). It is in that intersection you build a profitable and powerful proposition. Why? It is where the consumers will discover you as more than a faceless, cold corporation and see that you share the same values as them. In that intersection, you will transform yourself from a corporation to a corporation/person spilling out with human-like qualities.

Thinking in human terms is not easy for many technical, engineering-oriented companies. By becoming human, you employ not just the rational but the emotional parts of your corporate brain.

Are you ready to move from corporation to corporation/person?

To test my clients and see if they are ready to embrace the idea of corporation as person, I often ask them the following question:

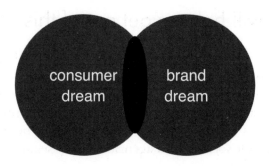

Figure 4.1   The magic happens in the intersection between the consumer dream and the brand dream

> If your company was a person, what kind of person would it be?

Oddly, this simple, straightforward question stumps nearly all my clients every time. They hesitate. They laugh. They stutter. They stumble around, finding it extremely difficult to conceive of their corporation as a human being.

We are not accustomed to thinking about our companies or brands in a human way. We cling to the almighty altar of rationality and suck the emotional life out of our businesses. Emotions are 'soft'. They don't count. Somehow they don't seem 'serious' or 'professional'. Let's face it. Emotions in a corporate setting make us squirm.

The irony, of course, is that our consumers have wanted to connect with corporations in a more human, more emotional way for many years. This is not new. Social media hasn't changed the fact that people want to connect in a more profound way. Social media has just pushed the issue to the forefront.

Consumers are sick of being treated like morons by cold, manipulative companies. They hate slick advertisements and slimy public relations campaigns, and prefer to believe the advice of fellow consumers over a corporate missive. It is the reason why users prefer to use peer-generated and peer-reviewed content than traditional company-developed articles. They greatly mistrust companies that say one thing and do the exact opposite.

Social media tap into a key global trend

I recently conducted a global trends study on security for the world's largest lock company, ASSA ABLOY. *The key finding was that for most people the true definition of security was to live in a world where they could connect with others in an authentic, real way. This emotional security was more important than any worries of physical security.*

Companies are not immune from these trends. Social media tools are just that – *tools*. But when tools correspond with larger trends touching people around the globe, they gain momentum and power. This is why social media represents such an important breakthrough.

Imagine you are a psychiatrist

If you are a psychiatrist, would you be troubled by the behaviour and psychology of many modern-day companies? Would you estimate that the bulk of companies have 'healthy' relationships with their consumers? Would you have advice to give those companies about their social skills?

In the past several decades, companies have deviated from the idea of being social. Some people would go so far as to say that many companies on the Fortune 500 can only be described as sociopaths in the sense they are utterly disengaged socially from their customers (Gary Koelling, Creative Director of Social Technology for Best Buy, quoted by Jessica Cameron-Ruud in TopRank Online Marketing blog). Our culture has let corporations get away with being antisocial for so long. Doing what they want, how they want, and shoving their point of view down people's throats. With not so much as an apology.

Let's go back again to the idea of a corporation as a person. Imagine you are at a cocktail party. Is your corporation/person someone you would want to talk to? Are they fun? Do they ask you questions, listen and care about what you say? Or are they just a loudmouth, talking about themselves all the time?

Just look at the millions of websites that litter the internet. Reams and reams of pages filled with companies talking about themselves. They barely mention their consumers. Or their consumers' problems. It's all about themselves. Me. Me. Me.

Is this self-centred, non-listening 'person' someone *you* want to do business with?

And – even more to the point – is this what *you* want to be?

Corporation/person as loudmouth simply doesn't work. Corporation/person as listener and as conversationalist is the way of the future.

Many corporations today are using social media as just another media tool. They lop off the word 'social' altogether. There is, of course, something bordering on the absurd about the antisocial using social media.

Social media is not a propaganda tool

The internet today should not be viewed as a propaganda tool. Propaganda implies manipulation. And as more and more people get involved in social media, the desire for authenticity grows. And authenticity is the exact opposite of manipulation.

Whatever you do, do not try to overly promote your company. This is a cardinal sin in social media. And it is one of the most common reasons why social media initiatives fail. When you promote yourself, the result is arrogant, uncaring communications. Blogs that aren't read. Videos that aren't played. Podcasts that are never listened to.

Authenticity is key

Authenticity. The quest for authenticity is nothing new. But as communication shifts from one-way monologues to two-way dialogues, the imperative to be honest and genuine is undeniable.

The good news is that when you are authentic, the pressure to be perfect is off. You can make mistakes. You are – after all – 'human'. You just can't skimp on authenticity.

Falseness, spin or manipulation won't be pardoned under any conditions. This theme will be reiterated throughout this book – whether it is copywriting on your web, posts on your blogs, viral marketing or social networking. The common thread is that authenticity is non-negotiable.

Find your true voice

Embrace the word 'social'. Listen to and follow your consumer. Try different tools, engage in different conversations. If you fail, that's

OK. Admit it, pick yourself up, brush yourself off and try something else.

Find your voice, your true voice. This is the biggest challenge. But it is well worth the effort.

Use trial and error

Social media is the new kid on the block. The internet in general is not much older. If the truth be told, no one really knows how best a company should employ online tools. So you need to be brave enough for a trial-and-error approach. Don't wait until you have the 'perfect' programme. You risk doing nothing at all. But if you experiment and have the courage to fail once in a while, you will get there. And in doing so, you will become a true corporation/person and your consumers will appreciate you for it.

How a corporation/person behaves

Let's take a closer look at the corporation/person.

A corporation/person empathizes and listens.

A corporation/person responds rather than observes.

A corporation/person emphatically rejects the notion that one size fits all. It realizes that its consumer base is nuanced, a conglomeration of multiple niches rather than one monolithic audience.

A corporation/person fully understands that the more you give, the more you get.

A corporation/person laughs.

A corporation/person expresses their individuality.

A corporation/person engages its consumers before selling to them. Engagement means your customer is involved with you, your company, your employees and your products.

A corporation/person embraces real-life emotions: hopes, dreams, disappointments and flaws.

The concept of corporation/person runs counter to everything we've been taught for decades. It defies the idea of being 'professional'. It wreaks havoc on the concept of keeping customers at arm's length.

For most companies, the concept of corporation/person is a hard idea to swallow. How can you be a corporation/person when you are supposed to be perfect and flawless? Companies like to gloss over everything they do with well-crafted corporate statements highlighting the good and downplaying the bad. Spin is the *règle du jour*, the norm.

Companies want to be perfect

Most companies are absolutely terrified if people see their flaws. Bad for sales. Bad for stock prices. Flaws = weakness = defeat = failure. Show the best, hide the worst. Everything needs to be processed and manipulated for public consumption, not unlike many of the products on the market today.

Market research is a case in point. When companies talk to their consumers, they often conduct 'focus groups'. These consist of the client hiding behind a one-way mirror and watching their consumers sitting around a table, being pummelled with questions about the client's products. The entire process is antiseptic and controlled. There is absolutely no contact between consumer and corporation – this would not be 'professional'.

In my work over the last 20 years, I have experimented with doing the exact opposite – with brilliant results. Instead of one-way mirrors, I plunk clients and consumers in the same room on a couch like 'real' people. An informal setting. Around a fireplace. Or even playing sports together. Furthermore, we never talk about products and their specifications. We talk instead about life, trends and values. Because it is the values that are the important drivers. *Not* the individual products. Apple hasn't built its success only on its product specifications; it has built its success on the values it represents.

This type of research yields rich results. Consumers and corporate representatives alike surprise each other as they discover their likes and dislikes and realize that behind the labels consumer and corporation are living, breathing human beings.

Upon reflection, my experiments in research contain many social media ingredients. Sharing, participation, being open. It's about prying the curtains open and revealing that the Wizard of Oz isn't the scary monster you thought he was – he's just another human being.

Social media is like a general store

Some describe social media as a giant revolutionary leap into the future. But maybe it's nothing more than a gentle step back to yesteryear.

Social media could lead us back to the days before big, giant corporations. Back to the days of the general store.

Perched proudly in the middle of Main Street, the general store was the centre of town activity and gossip. The jovial red-faced man and his wife were legend. They knew their clients by heart. As well as their friends, family, birthdays, anniversaries, personal preferences, desires, dreams, hopes and disappointments.

The general store invented the word 'social'. The owner of the general store had a knowledge and sensitivity about his consumer that most companies today can only dream about.

Social media, like the general store, can help you create personalized service to small niches as well as give you the ability to reach out with warmth, compassion and authentic humanity. Viewed this way, social media is a godsend as we seek to cement consumer relationships in an increasingly competitive world.

Examples of businesses who successfully use the new media

Are there examples of businesses who have successfully employed social media?

Circuit City is one such example. According to Jason Kleckner, Manager of Information Architecture for Target Corp, Circuit City leads in terms of live chat and customer feedback. By many accounts, they succeed in creating a real, consistent voice online by carefully appointing a designated representative to answer all customer/ prospect questions.

Ernst & Young is also named for their innovation in social media. Specifically, Ernst & Young uses social media as an agile recruiting tool. Ernst & Young was the first employer to use Facebook in this capacity, hiring more than 5,500 college students for entry-level positions and internships. Facebook was a good choice; it is one of the most popular sites among college students.

By maintaining this site, Ernst & Young proved they were not afraid to be transparent, a big step in building a good relationship with college students.

The company has sent a powerful message to students that Ernst & Young wants to listen to their needs, wants and desires. Furthermore, it puts Ernst & Young in an excellent competitive position. Recruiters continuing to use traditional recruiting methods appear to be one step behind.

Best Buy has applied social media to create an internal social networking site called BlueshirtNation. (A full explanation of BlueShirtNation can be found in Chapter 10, on social networking.)

Zappos, a company which sells shoes online, is famous for its heavy use of social media. This is an extraordinary company, well known for its humanity vis-à-vis both its employees and its consumers.

Integrating your interactive team

One of the issues corporations grapple with in terms of social media is who is in charge of it. There are many interested groups ranging from marketing to public relations to IT, not to mention your advertising agency and other outside vendors.

You will need to appoint a community manager. The reality is that in most organizations consumer relations isn't owned by one group. You have customer service, public relations or the brand manager. The community manager can come from any of these groups or be a spokesperson for all these groups.

Another challenge is the integration of your interactive team into the company. The team must have a voice and be involved as early as possible in the marketing process. In any event, your interactive team should be small and agile. What you build Monday morning could change completely by Tuesday afternoon.

The negative aspects of social media for a corporation

The fear of CEOs does have some basis. As *Business Week* pointed out on 16 April 2007:

> Trashing brands online can also be high theatre. Rats cruising around a Greenwich Village KFC/Taco Bell on YouTube. MySpacers busting their employers' chops. Faux ads bashing the Chevy Tahoe as a gas-guzzling, global-warming monster. Millions of people watch it. Is it any wonder companies lose control of the conversation?

Many corporations don't like social media because they are afraid of receiving negative comments. The idea of allowing millions of people to honestly express their opinion intimidates. What happens if a trickle of negative feedback turns into an avalanche? What happens if the negativity simply runs out of control?

Proponents of social media argue that if a company is willing and confident enough to receive negative feedback, it will only do the company good. It shows the company is open to listening, to change, to admitting mistakes and to having a real dialogue.

A company fearless enough to face its critics could indeed be viewed in a favourable light by consumers. For many, this is proof enough that the company is willing to be real and authentic. And that the company will engage in a true conversation and learn from comments rather than just shut down and arbitrarily shut off any such negativity.

In any event, according to one surprising study by BazaarVoice, the feedback that is given to companies is less negative than feared. In fact, a lot of feedback is given in the spirit of healthy dialogue in the hope that companies will improve their products and services:

- 90 per cent of reviewers said they wrote reviews to help others make better purchasing decisions;
- 70 per cent said they wrote reviews to help companies improve their products;
- 79 per cent wrote reviews to reward the company;
- 87 per cent wrote reviews that were generally positive.

In the same study, Brad Fay, Chief Operating Officer of the Keller Fay Group, says:

> Reviewers are motivated to help others and give back to the online community, not to knock down brands. In fact, online reviewers tell us they want to reward brands that perform well. This debunks a major myth about word of mouth and should encourage companies – and chief marketing officers – to be more comfortable with 'letting go' and inviting consumers to talk about their experiences.

What you need to do

So what do you need to do to use social media? You need to do all of the following:

- Be prepared to give up control of the message.
- Know the community you intend to participate in.
- Commit resources.
- Embrace business transparency.
- Create a social media marketing strategy. Set goals and objectives that can ultimately be related back to business outcomes; it is essential to be accountable.
- Start any new campaign by listening and observing first.
- Experiment with various programmes in little bits.
- Think content, content, content versus marketing, marketing, marketing:

  > What you need to do is, when you get involved in these blog posts or these chat rooms or these content-driven sites, you need to make sure you're coming from a place of content, not a place of marketing.
  >
  > Schefren, 2007

And to quote Rich Schefren again:

> By participating in a community, you not only build your brand but position yourself as an industry thought leader.
>
> Schefren, 2007

Remember: consumers are impressed by companies that take active roles in communities. And will like the brands and products such companies have to sell.

'Companies that are doing well with social media are being responsive, not just sitting back and watching', says Gary Koelling (Jessica Cameron-Ruud; see above).

The questions

Social media begs many questions.

How can we be efficient with social media? With traditional media, large companies built themselves around the idea of being efficient with big budgets, big campaigns, big audiences. But social media represents the exact opposite of efficiency: it is labour-intensive, non-standardized, and require participants to be highly involved.

How do you measure social media? How do you determine whether a campaign has been successful or not? What does a successful social media campaign look like? What about a healthy ROI? Unlike direct response marketing, which is about an event, social media are more about relationships. So the question really is: how do you measure the value of a relationship?

Measuring media has never been easy. For starters, you must initially think small. You don't need to invest $10 million. Social technology is inexpensive. Anyone who tells you otherwise is a bad adviser.

Begin by dipping your toe into social media and trying them in little bits. Experiment with a couple of tools. Don't swallow the whole whale at one time, otherwise you will get paralysed by huge budgets.

Having said all that, you can measure your results in several ways:

- RSS and newsletter subscribers;
- social bookmarks;
- blog comments;
- links to website by social media;
- monitoring referring links.

How do you deal with the speed of social media? Social media is slower than mass media. For example, the Blendtec guys had to work it a while before 'Will it blend?' went big. Viral hits like 'Elf yourself' didn't happen overnight. Companies used to working in mass media are used to immediate results. Social media is slow and steady, and it is a pace that many companies find frustrating.

Do you leap into social media? Or do you wait and watch and see what works and follow the crowds instead?

Jim Cuene, Director of Interactive at General Mills, is reported by Lee Odden in the TopRank Online Marketing blog as suggesting the following when you begin to experiment with social media:

- Fail fast and small.

- Pull the trigger slowly.

- Manage experimentation like a portfolio. Assume that if you conduct 10 experiments, one will work extremely well, two or three will be good qualified wins while at least one or two will be all-and-all failures.

- Work closely with companies like Facebook, MySpace, Google, Cafemom, Videoegg, Yahoo!, who will work with you to help create successes.

- Make sure you have the right resources behind any given project.

Should you even embark in the new media? If you can stomach the occasional negative remark and don't feel uncomfortable with open communications, the new media is for you. If you perceive social media as overly threatening, stay away from it altogether.

Never underestimate the amount of work which is required by new media. Are you interested in new media because it is 'hot'? Or have you actually established business objectives that make using the internet a sensible option?

No tool is a miracle worker

Don't forget that the tools in and of themselves are not miracle workers. The only miracle is a change in mindset – a change from corporation to corporation/person. It is only through that transformation that you will see results – and see whether or not the social media is there to help you.

It is no longer good enough to throw a message out, hoping it will stick. Now you are talking to real live human beings. You can't pull the wool over anyone's eyes. You need to be as human as the human beings who are your customers, your prospects, your employees and your vendors. No matter what your business. This is a huge – but not insurmountable – challenge for companies structured to deal with mass versus authenticity, spin versus real talk.

But when all is said and done, this is uncharted territory. Changing from corporation to corporation/person is hard, particularly for large companies. The nature of social media and the nature of big corporations remain – at least for the moment – diametrically opposed.

'There is a culture of participation and collaboration that companies need to adopt', Joe Schueller, IT Innovation Manager at Procter & Gamble, explains, according to Elizabeth Bennett in an article on the Baseline website. 'If any company with more than 500 employees has that figured out, I would be pretty impressed. This is all a grand experiment to find out whether social media can work in an environment that is, at the end of the day, hierarchical.'

5 The grand old lady of the internet

Maximizing the potential of your website

> A great website is an intersection of every other online initiative, including podcasts, blogs, news releases and other online media. In a cohesive and interesting way, the content-rich website organizes the online personality of your organization to delight, entertain and – most important – inform each of your buyers.
>
> Meerman Scott, 2007

For many people, websites *are* the internet. It's what they visit, where they go and – until the world of YouTube and Facebook appeared on the scene – our only way of having a web signature.

At last count, there are 156 million websites on the web (Amit Agarwal in posting on the website Digital Inspiration). Some of these websites were thrown up in a day. Others have cost hundreds of thousands of dollars, complete with all the bells and whistles that money can buy.

Despite all of this, websites are arguably the least understood and the most underutilized spaces on the web. Essential to anyone's global success, the vast majority of websites are nothing more than online brochure sites which drone on about organization missions, employee picnics, annual reports and directions to the company headquarters.

Getting your website right is the first and most crucial step in finding your voice on the internet. Despite its importance, though, it is odd that so few seem to get it right. If you succeed in transforming your website into the hard-working, interactive, vibrant vehicle it should be, you will find yourself way ahead of the pack.

What a website should be

Let's start with what a website should be.

First and foremost, a website should be at the front and centre of the action – bringing together many of the tools we discuss in this book. A website should be dynamic, interactive, engaging and vibrant.

Second, a website should sell. Even if you have created your website primarily to generate leads, a website must be a profitable contributor to the bottom line. That is why a website should never be a descriptive static document or online brochure. It is a selling tool.

Third, a website must engage and inform – because you must never forget a website is not there for you, your marketing department, your CEO or your webmaster. Your website must be wholly dedicated to your prospective consumers. It should be put up for your prospects and their problems. To captivate your prospects, a website must include exciting and ever-changing content, told in a unique voice.

Is your website a couch potato?

Most websites are nothing more than couch potatoes. Millions and millions of couch potatoes floating around in cyberspace. They sit around. They do very little. They describe the company. Half-heartedly sell. Have no interactive mechanisms. Don't even capture the names of the interested visitor. They are static and growing flabby, watching passively as the dynamic potential of the web floats by.

We need to ask why

The main reason there are so many ineffective websites is that no one dared to ask one simple question: why? Why put up a site in the first place? What is its purpose? What do we want to achieve with this site?

Like lemmings into the sea, we all jumped at one time or another into website mania with more or less the same template. Boring design. Little dynamic content. Droning on and on about ourselves rather than the problems our prospective clients face. So many websites. So many similar looks. And so often the same disappointing results.

How to fix things?

Identify the main purpose of your website

The first step is simply to ask why:

- Why am I putting this site up?
- What is its main purpose?
- What do I want my website to achieve?
- How is the website going to help my company with its bottom line?

So many people fail to ask these fundamental questions, delegating the task of website creation to their advertising agency or webmaster without fully thinking through the process.

Even if you already have a site, it is imperative that you step back and ask yourself the above questions. No matter what you have already invested in terms of time and money, if your website is just 'sitting there', then you have achieved nothing. You need to go back to square one.

Even if you want your website to multitask, your site still begs for a primary goal. You can then rebuild the design and content of your site to bring that goal into focus.

The more you ask your website to do in terms of quantity, the less it will be able to achieve in quality. So it is better to keep your website's focus as tight as possible.

Don't fill the void with bells and whistles

One of the problems with not establishing a clear purpose for your site is that the void is often filled with bells and whistles. Lots of technological wizardry and architecture. Flash. Splash pages. But the bells and whistles will never mask your site's lack of direction.

Far too much importance is placed on website design and technology. The vast majority of businesses spend far too much time concentrating on design rather than content. In other words, the accent has been on *how* the message is carried, rather than *what* the message should be.

Worship words instead

Words are, of course, the most powerful drug used by mankind.

Rudyard Kipling (1865–1936)

Words are the true currency of the web.

Veloso, 2004

The best websites focus primarily on content to pull together their various buyers, markets, media and products in one comprehensive place where content is not only king, but president and pope as well.

Meerman Scott, 2007

The content of the site – and its words – must become your absolute first priority. Not the design and the technology.

Unfortunately, most webmasters don't 'get' the importance of words. Their speciality tends to be the design and architecture of sites. But it is the words that woo the human beings who visit the site. If you want to hit a home run with your website, the words need to be top-notch all the way through.

The web is about words. Visitors come to read. The words need to be presented well in an easy-to-read manner so that the visitor can move forward through the site and the site's sales cycle.

People don't read, they scan

As you construct your web pages, keep in mind that reading is done very differently online. People *scan* text on the web, so do the following:

- Keep paragraphs short.
- Use plenty of white space.
- Use sans serif fonts such as Arial, Verdana and Helvetica.
- Don't vary font colours. Instead use (sparingly) techniques such as bold, italics, and italics and bold.
- Use images only when needed.
- Don't use coloured or tiled backgrounds.
- Black text on white or off-white background is easiest to read.

Headlines are king

Communicate your message quickly. The web is fast. Respect your visitor's time.

Headlines drive success. The first thing people see on the screen is your headline. As they move down the page, they scan the text looking for easy-to-read words (ie your subheads). Headlines and subheads tell the story and provide a quick summary of the entire page.

'Welcome to my home page' is not a headline. Seeing that, a visitor will leave immediately. Answer the prospective buyer's question: 'WIIFM – What's in it for me?' Explain the WIIFM in the headline.

Pull your reader seamlessly through the copy

Write one topic per content page. Keep the reader focused.

Write your copy using the inverted style of writing. Emphasize the most important concepts first.

Start with a headline. Then move to an opening paragraph which presents your conclusions first. The body copy should be divided into small paragraphs with one point per paragraph. Pull your reader into the copy with subheadings so as they scan they understand quickly what you are trying to say.

Be clear and concise

- Use clear, uncomplicated language.

- Use bullets to summarize content.

- Highlight with bold, italic or underlining.

- Present conclusions and key points first. Follow with less important information.

- Grab attention with captivating headlines.

- Write meaningful subheads.

- Present one idea per paragraph.

- Use boxes to set off testimonials, stories or case histories.

- Break up web copy into readable, bite-size chunks.

- Use short words and simple sentences.

- Use white space to pull people through the copy.

Write in a personal way, avoiding corporate language

> That way I can write copy the way I believe all copy should be written: as a conversation between two human beings rather than an announcement from manufacturer to consumer.
>
> Chris O'Shea, quoted in Crompton, 2000

The web is full of personal voices. Whether they are reading or writing, online users communicate in a very personal way.

When they arrive at a corporate website full of dry, formal and stiff language, they are so disappointed.

To stand out, you must talk in a personal way, even if you are a company. One to one.

Finding a unique voice that sets your company apart is a great challenge. And keeping that voice constant across all channels and media is no easy task.

Remember, people don't expect a 'personal' human being coming from a cold, faceless corporation. People don't expect the corporation/person. Exceed their expectations.

The web is littered with sites that drone on and on. Their voices are all the same: flat, dull and indistinct.

Don't let this happen to you. Success depends on creating a unique voice. As visitors interact with you, they should very quickly feel they know you as a company. Are you conservative? Playful? Fun? Irreverent?

Your unique voice doesn't need to be elaborate or super-creative. Your goal is simply to grab the attention of your visitors. And to stand out from the crowd.

A word about design

Every page of every website must have one primary design imperative: to showcase the message to its best possible advantage.

As unpopular as this idea may be to advertising agencies or IT specialists, the star of any site is its content, not its design or architecture. Design and architecture should support content discreetly and simply, not the other way around.

Check out eBay or Google as examples of big sites that are powerful in their simplicity (Figures 5.1 and 5.2). *Forget about the bells and whistles.* Keep everything simple, clean, intuitive and professional.

Use special effects sparingly. Avoid banners, animated gifs, buttons, multiple colour schemes, bandwidth-hogging graphics and Flash. All of these stand between the viewer and what they want most – information.

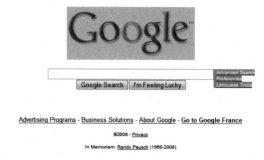

Figure 5.1   Google is an excellent example of the power of basic design

Websites are for buyers, not you

> Remember that your company is not the center of the universe for your customers. The site should be designed with customers' needs in mind and not to promote grandiose ideas of self-importance. Do not build a site that your top executives will love, they are not the target audience.
>
> Jakob Nielsen

Construct your site around the buyer – their problems and interests. Do *not* build your site around your organization and products.

For most companies, this advice may seem almost heretical. Not put our company and products first? Isn't the whole point to talk about ourselves?

It may be a bitter pill to swallow but your visitor does not come to your site to learn about you, your organization, its products or services. The visitor comes to the site because they have a problem and want it solved. Or they are looking for information. Because of this, your website must absolutely be organized around your customers' needs. Don't structure it around your perspective, organize it around their perspective.

First step? Identify your buyer personas

One way to organize your website around the customers' needs rather than your perspective is to identify, understand and articulate your customers' problems through 'buyer personas'.

Figure 5.2 eBay – keeping things simple

What is a buyer persona? 'A buyer persona profile is a short biography of the typical customer, not just a job description but a person description', says Adele Revella, who has been using buyer personas to market technology products for more than 20 years.

'A typical buyer personal profile includes information on his background, daily activities, problems, and the solutions for those problems. The more experience you have in your market, the more obvious the personas become', says David Meerman Scott in an article on the Web Ink Now website. A solid buyer persona guides you, allowing you to see the world through your consumer's eyes and to understand how they make buying decisions.

You don't want to construct a 'one size fits all' site. None of us has just one customer; we have several. Therefore it is better to construct a site around all the different types of buyers who are interested in your products. By doing this, you create a site built on content pertinent to each of your buyer persona needs versus building a site built around you, your organization and the way you see the world. These are two very different propositions.

David Meerman Scott, author of *The New Rules of Marketing and PR*, gives some examples of buyer personas:

- Look at universities. One buyer persona would be prospective students. Another buyer persona would be the parents who are not only key decision makers but pay the bills. Both are interested in universities but their problems and questions are very different.

- A software provider has many different buyer personas: the technologist, the user of the application or the business buyer.

- A consultant might need a page for meeting planners that are interested in hiring him for speaking engagements. Another buyer persona would be the companies interested in hiring him for his advice.

Meerman Scott, 2007

You need to identify your target audience in detail: their problems, their solutions, their hopes and dreams. Each buyer persona needs to be understood inside and out. Once you understand this, you can create specific, on-target content.

Before you write a single word, know everything there is to know about your customer. Create an intimate portrait. Give each buyer persona a first name. Roger. Susan. Gail. Know *why* you gave them that name. You should feel like you know them as real people – like they are your best friends. If you can do this, you will write to an audience of one, rather than to an audience of the masses.

This is an absolutely fresh way of thinking about your site's design. It is also a very coherent way of organizing your content. You use your buyer personas as a starting point, constructing both content and design around each persona. By doing this, you can lead your consumers through the sales cycle on your site in an effective, meaningful way.

Let's break this process down into discrete steps:

1. Define your consumer. Break your consumer profile down into distinct 'buyer persona' categories.

2. Fully understand each discrete consumer profile.

3. Identify the individual problems and concerns of each buyer persona.

4. Write content that addresses those problems and concerns.

Provide clear links from your content to where you ask for an action. That action could range from something as simple as signing up for an e-newsletter to purchasing a product.

Don't let your visitors get lost

Navigation is important. If the idea is to get your visitor to read your site's content, walking seamlessly through the site's sales cycle, it is imperative your visitor doesn't get lost.

From many visitors' perspective, sites suffer from two inherent problems.

First problem is that when you read websites, you can only see one page at a time. You can't flip through a site like a brochure. You can't take in a site with a single glance. You can only see one page at a time. You don't know what is going to happen next. For that matter, visitors often don't remember where they have just been.

Second problem is that every website is set up differently. Every new visitor is at least initially 'lost'. They don't know how you have put your site together and fumble about to get their bearings at the beginning.

Once again, don't forget the cardinal rule. Keep your visitor's needs first and foremost. Spend less time on how *you* might like to organize your site and more time building a site in an intuitive and logical way for new visitors.

Headings, subheads and links all need to be descriptive and crystal clear. Create simple pathways through your site so visitors can easily find what they are looking for.

Design every page as if it is the first page your visitor will see

A second navigational concern is related to where people land when they arrive at your site.

You build a home page which clearly identifies the site's key topics with clear descriptions of how to move forward. But what happens if your visitors don't arrive on the home page? You can't control where they will land. Search engines, blogs and even other sites can easily link into your interior pages.

In a way, the idea of a home page is nothing but an artificial construct. Home pages are the internet equivalent of the front page you would see on a magazine, newspaper or book.

But there is no guarantee your visitor will arrive at your home page. You must design and write copy for *every* page on your site in the knowledge that it may be the first page people see when they arrive at your site.

Every interior page should include site-wide navigation tabs and links. Headlines, subheads and links should be designed in the knowledge that your visitor may be better served elsewhere on the site. *In other words, apply home page thinking to every page on your site.*

You therefore must always balance two navigational issues.

On the one hand, the pathway from your home page needs to be very clear and logical. Moving people from your home page to a second-level page requires discipline and is essential if you want a smooth-working website that converts visits into sales.

On the other hand, visitors who arrive directly on an interior page are just as important to your website's success. Think about what those visitors want. Write headlines and text that include them.

In conclusion, every page is a landing page. Every page serves two audiences: those who arrive from your home page and those who arrive directly from some outside link.

Be sure your first impression is a good one

First impressions count.

When you 'meet' a website for the first time, it is just like meeting a real person. People make snap judgments; it takes them less than 10 seconds to decide what they think about you. Even less time when they arrive at your website. First impressions in a blink of an eye. Don't lose visitors before you have begun.

The purpose of your website should shout out when people arrive. Immediately illustrate the value of your site. Persuade them with one succinct glance they should stay.

Given the importance of the first impression, it is not surprising that the first screen is the prime selling space of your website. Whatever you put in that first screen will make or break you.

The first screen is *not* the first page (ie the home page or the landing page). The first screen is just the part of the page that appears on the screen when you land on the website – before you scroll down or sideways.

Don't make the classic mistake of splashing a large logo or company name in gigantic letters on the screen. An oversized logo simply wastes valuable selling space.

Conversely, a headline *must* be included in the first screen. Headlines reign king. A website without a headline is like a rider without a horse. It's pointless. Millions of websites are guilty of forgetting about the all-important headline.

Answer the 'What's in it for me?' question

A well executed website is like a good TV programme or film. Content and delivery work hand in hand to captivate.

The way forward is easy. As we have discussed, start with a site navigation that is organized with your buyers in mind, rather than your company's organization. Be sure you understand the buying process in detail. This will help create more effective web content.

Your potential relationship with a customer begins the second he or she hits your home page or landing page. He or she wants and needs to see a reflection of him- or herself. It is for this reason that you organize your site with content for each distinct buyer persona.

Identify situations in which each buyer persona may find him- or herself. Answer their questions, resolve their problems. Also, different people like to see content in different ways. Augment text with photos, audio and video content.

The sooner the website answers the eternal customer question 'What's in it for me?' the better the results.

A website which is organized around your buyers rather than your organization is a fresh way of thinking. It will drive all your website activities. It will shake your website loose and give it energy and vitality.

Hook buyers in from the start. Hang onto them until the sale is complete.

Individuals go to sites to look for information. They don't go to sites looking for advertising. By providing information when they need it, you begin to create a long and profitable relationship.

The vast majority of sites fail to realize their potential. How do you know if your website works or not? A great website is one in which your prospect can trust and believe.

You build trust and credibility through your content. Writing excellent content warms up your prospect, putting them in an 'open to buy' mindset.

Complement copy with other interactive content

Complement copy with non-text content: photos, audio feeds, video clips, cartoons, charts and graphs which inform and entertain. Avoid generic stock photos as they feel false and manufactured. Be wary of building a large image site or using distracting multimedia like Flash. Eye candy often detracts from your main job of communicating well.

Engage visitors. Get them involved with your website's content. By building their interest, you gently move them through the sales cycle. Examples of interactive activity include stock quoting and charting applications found on financial sites or 'e-mail your politician' on political advocacy sites. Never forget to include an easy-to-find 'contact us' button and direct feedback mechanisms like 'rate this website' buttons, online forums, viewer reviews or a comments section.

Another interactive tool well-suited for a website is a forum or wiki (a website that allows people to collaborate together by adding, removing and even editing content). Customers can share with one another within a vibrant community of like-minded people. An enthusiastic group of customers interacting with each other on your site translates into great marketing.

RSS is an exciting new website tool

RSS is another underutilized asset.

Did you know that over 64.7 per cent of all the business e-mail you send is not even opened, let alone read?

Enter RSS. RSS stands for Really Simple Syndication and Rich Site Summary. RSS is simple. It is free to use. Your clients (and you) will never have to endure the perennial problems of spam and filter. It gets your content delivered directly in front of your subscribers, prospects and customers whenever you want and how often you want. In other words, it means that 100 per cent of your marketing message is delivered.

How exactly does RSS work? A website's content often changes frequently. Examples of such websites are news sites, weblogs or product information pages. For a visitor, it would be very tedious to keep coming back to each of these sites to check if there is new content. With RSS, the website author maintains a list of notifications on the website. These notifications are called RSS feeds. People who are interested in the latest changes will check this list. Even better, special computer programs called RSS aggregators automatically access the RSS feeds of the websites you care about and will organize the results for you.

Producing an RSS feed is very simple, and major websites now provide this feature, including major news organizations like the New York Times, the BBC and Reuters, as well as many weblogs.

The advantage of RSS is that your customers receive only what they ask for. Unlike e-mail, there is no spam. What is delivered is controlled completely by the consumer.

RSS is the powerful web tool which revolutionizes the distribution of information to consumers. For marketers, RSS gives a fantastic opportunity to connect directly with their consumers and build trust and loyalty with their audiences. For consumers, RSS gives them complete control over the flow of information they receive. If the quality of their feed declines, they can simply remove it, no longer receiving content from that source.

It is certain that RSS will become a standard – just like e-mail addresses and websites are now a must for businesses.

RSS strategies help you get a loyal following of community members who regularly read, listen to or view your content. They don't need to seek you out. Instead the content is delivered to them. Interested consumers subscribe to your blog, getting the latest updates via portals that aggregate postings like Technorati, NewsGator, Google Reader and many more, or have the entries sent directly to them via e-mail services like FeedBlitz and FeedBurner.

Here are some RSS strategies suggested by Kim Roach (Solis and Livingston, 2007):

1. Get a FeedBurner service so that people can receive e-mail from you.

2. Submit your site to RSS directories and content aggregators.

3. Add a large RSS button to your site.

4. Have RSS links at the bottom of each content entry.

5. Offer an e-mail newsletter in addition to RSS. An e-mail newsletter allows you to form a closer relationship with your visitors and picks up those who still aren't comfortable with RSS technology.

RSS provides companies with a powerful information management tool and avoids the increasingly overcrowded and spam-ridden e-mail channel. Only a tiny sliver of organizations use RSS for syndicating news and content. Even fewer understand that RSS feeds are the perfect vehicle to market to niche customers. Any content that can be broken down into chunks such as news releases, blog postings or product updates can be syndicated via RSS.

In Table 5.1 and Figure 5.3, you can see the international growth in RSS consumption. While it has made significant inroads in some countries, the RSS wave is just beginning to swell.

Table 5.1 Usage of RSS is growing around the world

Subscribing
Consuming content: RSS (%)

	Sep 06	**June 07**	**Mar 08**
Global	16	15	34
France	28	11	26
Germany	5	8	27
Italy	7	16	25
Russia	28	18	57
Spain	19	13	34
UK	10	9	25
USA	14	9	17

Source: Universal McCann

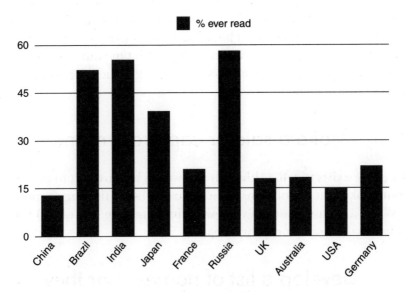

Figure 5.3   The use of RSS feeds is a global trend

The beauty of permission marketing

With a tool like RSS, you enter into the realm of what Seth Godin calls 'permission marketing'.

> The name of this game is to get your prospects to point to themselves as hot prospects. They literally agree to learn more about your company and its benefits...The first and main rule in permission marketing is that it truly is based on selfishness: prospects will grant you permission to market to them only if they know exactly how they'll benefit.
>
> J Conrad Levinson, 2007

When your readers subscribe to your RSS feeds, they give you 'permission' to tell them more. About you. About your market. About your service and expertise. This, as you can appreciate, is an amazing opportunity in this crowded, cluttered world. On your side, however, you *must* consistently deliver quality content. Otherwise, your 'loyal' subscriber will be no more.

Make a sale or capture a name

A website exists to sell. (Although you would be hard put to prove this point looking at the millions of lacklustre websites floating around).

When a visitor comes to your site, aim at getting one of two things. Either make a sale or capture a name.

Develop a list of names... or they vanish forever

The first indispensable step in making a website work – and sell – is to capture names.

Developing a list of names is of crucial importance.

It is very difficult (and very rare) to convert web visitors into customers during their first website visit. Why should they convert? They don't know you. They are not familiar with your products.

Research shows that a potential customer may view your offer as many as seven or more times before purchasing a product. Before they are ready to take their credit card out, you need to talk with these potential customers. Without their names, such a conversation is impossible.

Many web marketing strategies depend on visitors voluntarily coming back to a website. Forget it. If they click away, they click away forever.

You need inbound and outbound strategies

No internet marketing plan is complete unless it embraces inbound and outbound strategies.

Inbound traffic is what you do to get your customer to your website. You generate inbound traffic through a variety of methods including advertising, article writing or search engine optimization.

E-mails, e-newsletters or RSS give you outbound traffic. Outbound traffic maintains a dialogue with customers, giving them information and promotional offers.

Both inbound and outbound strategies are necessary for an effective website.

But an outbound strategy cannot exist without names. Therefore it is absolutely essential that you capture the e-mail addresses of interested website visitors. No names, no customers and... no sales.

Your visitor most likely ended up on your website while casually surfing the web. So you need to get their name, introduce yourself and get a relationship going before any sale can be made. This is simple common sense.

So what's the best way to get those names? In today's world, where people jealously guard their right to privacy, they won't give away their names and e-mail addresses for nothing. They will give you those names if they get something of value (like a compelling, informative e-newsletter) in exchange.

Enter the e-newsletter

What is an e-newsletter? It is a content-rich newsletter sent daily, weekly or monthly to your opt-in list in an effort to build long-lasting, trusting relationships with your customer base. While it can carry the occasional promotional message, it should first and foremost deliver highly valuable, information-rich content. Create an e-newsletter which is a must-read for your customer.

An e-newsletter builds trust between you and your potential customer. Trust is in short supply on the internet. This is a medium where, more often than not, your prospect doesn't know you. They can't see you. They can't talk to you directly.

By far the easiest way to establish trust is to publish an e-newsletter in which you consistently demonstrate you are competent and willing to solve consumer problems.

Another benefit of the e-newsletter is its ability to cement relationships with current customers. The ongoing goodwill of your current customers is important to your future. Staying in touch by e-newsletter is the best way to do that.

An e-newsletter is a place where you can tell your readers (both existing and potential customers) about a special purchase which enables you to give buyers a big price reduction.

An e-newsletter also presents you as a thought leader. You can share industry knowledge, market trends or new techniques.

In sum, you are just a click away from meaningful contact with your clients and prospects by e-newsletter.

People go online to find information

People go online to find information. Even if they are shopping for something, they are still looking for information, not advertising. Contrary to popular myth, the internet is not just one big advertising slot. *The internet is a place where people go to seek information.*

A study conducted by web usability experts John Morkes and Jakob Nielsen showed that web users 'detest anything that seems like marketing fluff or overly hyped language, and prefer factual information'.

This means that web copy needs to have an editorial feel. It cannot and should not feel like a sales pitch. Even if you are selling, your sales pitch should not sound like an ad but should read more like an editorial, testimonial, advice, case study or endorsement.

People tune out ads, but they tune in editorial information.

Making a sale is not an isolated event

A customer purchase is the result of a complete experience with you. Don't change your online voice just as you make a sale. You can't have a passive site and then expect one screen of tough selling to make the sale. The entire customer experience with you should support the sale.

The most successful sites take into account the buying cycle when writing content. It is essential to develop content that links visitors through the cycle to the point of purchase. Unfortunately, the vast majority of sites don't do this; they are little more than online brochures or one-way advertising. As such, these sites are completely ineffective as sales tools.

Design your website with the buying cycle in mind

Buyers considering a purchase undergo a certain thought process. That process could last a few minutes, an hour, days, weeks or months. For example, a business-to-business sales cycle can involve many buyer personas and could take up to a year to complete.

Buyers at the beginning of the sales cycle need basic information about how an organization can solve their problems. This is the point in the process where you can give more information in the form of e-newsletters, webinars or podcasts.

As the buyer moves along the sales cycle, your prospect may need to compare products and services. Your prospect looks more closely for the full benefits of your offer and how that offer stacks up against those of your competitors.

As the customer approaches the end of the buying process, you must provide tools that facilitate the sale: for example, online demonstrations or a tool that allows your prospect to enter specific details about requirements and then suggests the appropriate product.

Equally, the buyer at the end of the cycle will need easy-to-use purchase mechanisms linked directly to the content so they can easily complete the purchase.

The buying cycle doesn't end with the purchase. Once the sale is made, it is very important that you continue your online dialogue with the new customer. For example, you can create a mechanism which allows customers to give you feedback. Or you can establish a customer-only community where the buyer can interact with other customers or key employees in your organization.

Ask for the order; ask for action

The majority of sites are oddly passive. Product descriptions sit passively. E-mail address sign-up boxes for newsletters appear without words to encourage people to sign up. Home pages show content but make no effort to drive people deeper into the site.

You must be clear and explicit as you steer your prospect through the website.

Write strong copy at all the site's potential action points. Ask for the order. Make it easy for a prospect to buy or sign up for an e-newsletter.

Close the sale. Remind your visitor of all the great reasons why your product or service is such a great deal. Write strong sales copy that encourages your visitor to make the purchase right now. Repeat your guarantee. Give a freephone number that people can call.

Five questions which distil the online sales process

Maria Veloso, a world-renowned web copywriting expert, has written a guideline comprising five questions that distil the buyer persona/ sales process:

1. What is the problem?

2. Why hasn't the problem been solved?

3. What is possible? Paint a picture of the way things will be when your prospect's problems are solved.

4. What is different now? Explain who you are and how your product/service can help them. Discuss your Unique Selling Proposition. A USP sets your product or service apart from

those of all other competitors, giving your prospect a compelling reason to buy.

5.   What should the prospect do now, eg sign up, pick up the phone, register, opt-in, buy the product or services?

A list of dos and don'ts

Dos

- Be honest.

- Know your products well.

- Make your offerings in context, within the natural flow of your content.

- Outline weaknesses of your product or service. Buyers will trust you more if you are objective.

- Pre-sell your visitor with high-value information that fosters trust and gives you credibility. Give your visitor solutions to their problems. Your prospect will like and respect you because of this positive experience and be in an open mindset to buy.

- Make it easy for people to find what they are looking for.

- Tell them enough about your product so they are comfortable paying the price you are asking.

Don'ts

- Don't be desperate. Don't hit visitors over the head with offers. No one wants to be aggressively pitched.

- Don't be 'you-focused'. Starting with the creation of your buyer personas, you should always be customer-focused.

- Don't be pushy.

- Don't put up a site just to sell. Put up a site to deliver information.

Summary

- The website is where all the pieces of the puzzle come together – it is where you put forth your online personality.
- The website is not static but should be ever-changing and dynamic.
- The website is a place to sell; don't squander such precious real estate.
- Capture names or make a sale; don't let your visitors vanish forever.
- Send out a content-rich e-newsletter once a week or once a month; it will be a great way to build relationships and increase the ROI on your website.

6 Googling it

Mastering search engine optimization so that your business can stand out

I would now like to turn to the topic of search engine optimization. Never has there been a topic more misunderstood, obsessed over or feared. And for all the experts who fixate over this subject, there are millions more individuals, companies and websites that don't even know it exists.

One thing is certain in all the confusion. The voice of search engine optimization is one of the most powerful in the online marketing choir.

A definition of search engine optimization

So what exactly is search engine optimization (or SEO, as it is commonly called)? At its very simplest, search engine optimization is defined as:

> The use of search engines to draw traffic to a website. It's the technique of attaining a higher ranking in search engines and directories via alteration of website code and copy to make [the website] more search-engine compatible.
>
> Kalena Jordan, on search engine optimization wiki

Search engines sit at the internet's epicentre

But before we can understand how to optimize for the search engines, we need first to review the idea behind search engines.

The search engine in effect is a key driver of all that happens on the internet because it is the number-one way internet users find information.

Search engines are nothing short of a marketer's dream.

Search engines are pure magic

A search engine works simply. A prospective client types in a keyword or set of keywords to find out more about any given subject. And the search engine delivers an instant response – thousands of websites that contain content on the precise subject in which the viewer is interested.

The search engine turns the marketing rules of the last 100 years upside down. Instead of having to mass-market with television or magazine advertisements, you can intersect with your consumer on the web at the precise moment they are interested in learning more about your market or product.

Pure magic.

The ten most wanted spots in search engine results

So, what's the hang-up? The problem lies in the fact that a query on a search engine can turn up thousands – even millions – of matching web pages. But only the ten most relevant matches are displayed on the first page.

Everyone, of course, wants to be on that first page. Everyone wants to be counted among the top ten results. Most users will find a result they like in the top ten. If you are number 11, you may get missed altogether (see Figure 6.1).

Studies show that 62 per cent of search engine users click on a search result within the first page of results. Ninety per cent of users click on a result within the first three pages (iProspect website, 2006). So if you want the marvel of the search engines to work for you – if you want to

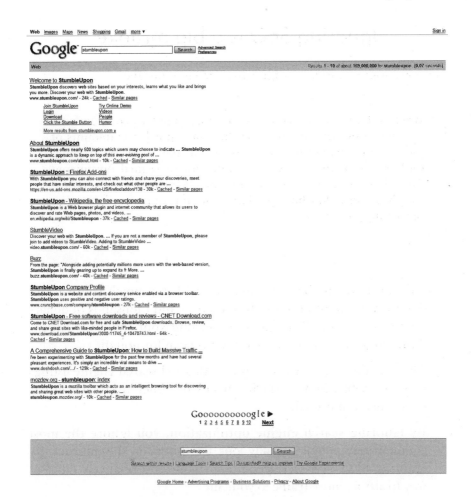

Figure 6.1 The all-important Google top ten

intersect with the consumer at the exact moment they are looking for your products or services – there is an urgent need for your website to rank within the first three pages of search results or, even better, on the first page.

And getting to that coveted top ten position will be near impossible if you don't employ some kind of search engine optimization tactics.

Oddly enough, millions of companies and their websites ignore SEO. Companies spend thousands of dollars on online and offline advertising. They invest in banner ads, pay–per-click advertising or viral marketing. Yet they ignore search engine optimization. Either they don't know it exists or they don't think it's important.

Ignoring SEO is a big mistake

Here are some reasons why ignoring SEO is a mistake:

> Brick and mortar companies don't refuse to put a sign up in front of their businesses just because they have put large amounts of money into promoting themselves via television advertising. Online companies, likewise, should not disregard optimizing their sites for search engines – a relatively inexpensive exercise – simply because they have put large amounts of money into other marketing strategies.
>
> Jordan, 2008

- You can have the best website ever, with top-notch content and design. You can put hundreds of hours – and thousands of dollars – into its creation. But if no one can find your site, your expenditure in terms of time and money has been for nought.

- The equation is simple. A website with good search engine listings is more visible. More visibility means healthier traffic. Healthier traffic means more sales.

- By ignoring search engine optimization, you ignore the most common way people actually look for things on the internet. By ignoring SEO, you sacrifice an enormous and relatively efficient way to attract more traffic to your site.

- Visitors who get to your site via a search engine are by definition more qualified leads and more likely to buy than your average visitor. This is simple logic. If someone conducts a search for certain keywords and phrases directly related to your products or services, they will match with you and be far more open to your offering.

- SEO provides a great return on investment. Shari Thurow, author of *Search Engine Visibility*, says:

  > Because millions of people use the search engines and directories to discover websites, maximizing your site's search engine visibility can be a powerful and cost-effective part of an online marketing plan. A properly performed search engine marketing campaign can provide a tremendous long-term

return on investment (ROI). Personally, I have witnessed many sites receiving millions of dollars in increased sales within months of launching a search engine-friendly website.

Thurow, 2007

The bottom line is this. If you build a website, you need to use SEO. You need to be sure that when your visitors look for you, they find *you*, not one of your competitors.

Search engine optimization should be at the top of the list of priorities for any company with a web presence.

How search engines work

There are many different types of search engines. But basically internet users use two types of search sites: search engines or directories.

There are search engines...

A search engine crawls the web, using special software called a robot or spider that automatically follows links, indexing web pages which are then added to the search engine's database. As it follows each page, it stores away copies of the code and the keywords found in that code. These codes and keywords will be compared against search queries later on. Depending on the search engine, web crawling and re-crawling occurs between every one to three months. Google is the classic example of a search engine.

... and there are directories

A directory, on the other hand, is a database of web pages which is manually collected or reviewed by real people. Open Directory is an example of one such directory.

Some search sites combine the search engine principle with the directory idea. Yahoo! is a good example of such a combination. MSN Search is another example.

The ranking codes of search engines

When an internet user types in a search query (a word or phrase), the search engine makes a relevant match with a web page that contains similar keywords. Those web pages that are considered the most relevant will logically be shown at the top of the search engine results. The best results turn up on the first page and earn the coveted spot of the top 10.

The burning question for everyone is: how do the search engines select which pages are the most relevant?

Each search engine has its own formula which determines the relevancy of one website over another. When matching sites with search queries, search engines assign weight to each web page based on how closely the page content matches their formula.

This mathematical formula is called an algorithm. The algorithm is a much-guarded secret, can be based on over 100 different factors, and is changed on a regular basis. The algorithm is extremely complex and nearly impossible to crack.

Understanding the search engines' algorithms

But at their very simplest, the search engines tend to search for the following three things: keyword density, keyword prominence and link popularity.

Keyword density

Search engines look for how many of the terms in the search query are actually found on the page. Pages with more terms matching the query tend to rank higher. But it goes beyond simply having the terms in your copy. Keyword density is critical. Pages with around 7 per cent of the words matching the query are considered good matches. Not any more (the search engines don't like websites that stuff themselves with keywords and phrases), but not any less.

Keyword prominence

Search engines will also analyse *where* on the page the keywords are placed. Query terms need to appear in important places such as the following:

The title

The title tag is crucial to your SEO success. According to SEO expert Danny Sullivan of Search Engine Watch, 'The text you use in the title tag is one of the most important factors in how a search engine may decide to rank your web page' (article on SearchEngineWatch.com).

And according to HighRankings.com, title tags are definitely one of the 'big three' in terms of the algorithmic weight given to them by search engines; they are as important as your visible text copy and the links pointing to your pages – perhaps even more so.

Given this, it is extremely important for websites to have different keywords and phrases relating to the site content included within the title tag on each page. These keywords should be integrated either as a replacement for or an addition to the company name or page title.

Headings and emphasized text

Most search engines give more weight to terms found in bold headings and in italicized or coloured text.

Body text

Body text includes all the words that appear on the page. Body text that appears closer to the top of the page is considered to be higher in priority than text found in the middle or bottom of the page.

Search engines cannot 'read' graphics or images, only text. However, they *can* index the text descriptions that Alt IMG tags provide. Alt IMG attributes are places in the HTML code where you can enter a text description for a graphic or image that appears on a web page. Alt IMG attributes are important because they can greatly contribute to a site's relevancy for particular search queries.

Description

Web pages generally contain a summary that some engines still show under the title in the search results. This is called the meta description tag. Search engine robots gather this information when indexing websites and often use it when referencing web pages in the search listings.

While not all search engines continue to utilize the meta description tag, a majority of search engines rely on the content of this tag to provide information about a site that they can match with search queries.

To give a website the best ranking possible, it is highly recommended that each page of the site include a unique title tag and unique meta tags, individually tailored to the content of that specific page.

The use of tailored title and meta tags on each page creates multiple entry points to a website. In other words, it enables relevant content to be found in search engines no matter where it resides on a site. For example, instead of relying on visitors to arrive via the home page, the optimization of individual site pages makes each page more visible in the search engines, providing additional gateways to the site's content. The more pages optimized, the wider the range of keywords and phrases that can be targeted and the more entry points are created to a site.

Link popularity

Link popularity – the number of sites (and relevancy of these sites) linking to a given site – is a very important factor in the ranking algorithms of many search engines.

Link popularity can be defined as the number of sites (and relevancy of these sites) linking to a given site. The more links you have pointing to your site, the more traffic you'll receive. The more relevant links you have pointing to your sites, the higher your site's link popularity.

Link building is essential in the search engine optimization process but many people overlook it. Implementing a link building campaign will help improve your site's link popularity, increase your site traffic and ultimately improve your search engine ranking.

Links are not equal. Every website on the internet is given a calculation of its authority or intrinsic value, which is based on the links that come to it. Sites that are linked to high-authority sites become higher in the authority chain themselves.

Your success or failure rests on good keyword research

So the big three in the search engine algorithms are keyword density, keyword prominence and link popularity. It is logical therefore that when you seek to optimize your site, you absolutely must understand what the keywords and phrases are that your visitors are most likely to use. The process of finding these keywords and phrases is called keyword research.

In search engine optimization, nothing happens without good keyword research. The success or failure of your search engine marketing begins with your keyword research. Keyword research is how you reach precise target markets. Figure out what words those niche markets will use to reach you and you have won half the battle.

To quote Brad Hill, author of *Building Your Business with Google for Dummies*, 'If you're not dreaming of keywords at night, you're not optimizing enough. Keywords are the thread that runs through the entire SEO process from start to finish' (Hill, 2004).

The sad fact is that far too many companies don't give enough thought to the keywords they use. Wrong keywords mean you are targeting the wrong audience. Even if you *do* have excellent rankings, those rankings are worthless if they are based on incorrect keywords.

When you select the keywords for your sites, always select search terms that describe your products in the most specific, simple and logical way possible. This will ensure that you increase traffic to your site but *also* that the visitors who arrive there are highly qualified to buy your products and services.

This is the process you need to go through as you select your keywords.

1. Understand your target market.

2. Write down those markets you are targeting.

3. Create a preliminary list of keywords. Get inside the head of your target market. Imagine the words *they* would use to find you.

4. Add qualifying terms that will help you define your market even more closely. In other words, if you have a hair salon in New York city, a qualifying term would be 'New York'. An even more precise qualifying term might be 'Upper West Side New York'. Qualifying terms help increase the visitor conversion rate while reducing the click-away rate considerably.

5. Ask friends and family what keywords or search phrases they would type in. Add these words to your list.

6. Analyse competitors' websites and see what keywords they are using.

7. Use a keyword research tool such as Keyword Discovery or WordTracker to help brainstorm keywords. You can also use the Yahoo! Keyword Selector Tool or the Google Keyword Suggestion Tool to find more keywords.

8. Build your list until you have twice the number of keywords/ phrases you think you will need. Most pages can only be optimized for a maximum of two or three keywords/phrases. Therefore, if your website has 10 pages, you will need around 60 keywords/phrases altogether.

9. Assess the popularity of your keyword choices. How many site matches appear for your keyword searches? Of the top 30 results, how many have optimized their sites? Can you do better?

10. Refine your list. Always keep your audience in mind.

11. Be simple, logical and straightforward.

12. Don't be too generic. Choose words that are highly targeted to your precise business. The more qualified your site visitors are when they arrive at your site, the more likely you will be able to convert those visitors into paying customers.

13. Identify different target words for different pages.

14. Keywords and phrases should always be at least two or more words long. These phrases will give you a better shot at success.

15. Build your copy around your keywords and not the other way around. If your existing page copy doesn't contain any of your target search keywords, you're going to have to rewrite it.

The magic of SEO copywriting

Search engines are blind. In other words, they are text readers and do not have the ability to see any images at all. When indexing websites to store in their database, search engine robots rely on the text content of a site to tell them what the site is all about.

Writing SEO-friendly copywriting is therefore crucial to your success.

Let me repeat. Search engines rely on the text in websites to provide information about site content. It is this text-based information which is then compared with search queries. To find a site which matches a search query, the search engine *must* find the keywords used in that query somewhere on the site.

The easiest way to ensure your site is relevant to any given search query is to include logical keywords/phrases within the text on the web pages.

The web is plagued with sites selling particular items without once making reference to those items in their site text. Another mistake is to include a lot of marketing speak like 'internet solutions' or 'superior services' – keywords and phrases that the potential customer is highly unlikely to type in.

Search engine listings and human searches are based on the language people use when looking for something online. However, the language used by business owners and web groups may be very different.

For instance, a company may want to say, 'We deliver an integrated suite of digital printing solutions.' On the other hand, someone looking for printing services may type into a Google search something like 'brochure printing'. Will Google send brochure printing searchers to that company's digital printing solutions page? Probably not.

Sites lacking any keyword research tend to use very generic, unfocused body copy or sales-oriented hype. Neither style contributes to high search engine rankings.

Writing excellent search engine-friendly copy is an art. You must ensure that your keywords/phrases are integrated seamlessly. The text must flow smoothly for the reader.

Put text into the site that your visitor will appreciate, like and find informative. Never write your copy with the search engines in mind and the algorithms. Algorithms do not make inquiries or purchases. People do.

If your copy is attractive and readable and encourages real people to contact you or buy a product, then it is highly likely to be equally attractive to the search engine. When writing your copy, you should not be trying to sell your product or services with blatant over-the-top advertising. Be more subtle. You are fulfilling a wish or a need or solving a problem, so be informative. People have carried out a specific search, so the need is already there. You now have to give them the information they need to convince them to buy. The content is the key to making sales as well as attracting the attention of the search engines.

Here are some guidelines:

- Don't compromise the readability of your copy. Hire an expert copywriter to strike the right balance between keyword integration and readability. Extreme skill is needed when combining keywords with convincing copy.

- Never lose sight of the reader when writing your body copy.

- Write at least 250 words of visible body text on each page.

- Be emotive.

- Use easy-to-grasp concepts.

- Be simple.

- Describe your product or service well.

- Show the reader how your product or service will make them feel or improve their lives.

- Always build your page copy around your keywords. Don't do it the other way around.

- If your website is about dogs, talk about dogs. Not pets.

- Avoid excess repetition.

- Keep large chunks of text to a minimum. Use bullet points, white space, graphics, lists and subheadings to break text up. This makes it easier to read.

Avoid Flash

Adobe Flash (previously known as Macromedia Flash) animations and splash pages are extremely popular, particularly on the websites of larger companies on the internet. The bigger the brand, the bigger the budget. The bigger the budget, the more complex the Flash image.

Flash is just the latest in an obsession with visuals on the web. And this obsession is often at the expense of site content which is much more search engine-friendly.

Copywriter Heather Lloyd-Martin emphasizes this in her article 'Copy sells, Flash doesn't – implications for search engine optimization' (published on SuccessWorks website):

Let's say you're visiting a retail store. The store is the latest in hip, with flashing lights and rock videos pounding from every corner. You see a product, love it, but have a few questions about it. You wait for a sales person... and wait... and wait... and still your questions aren't answered. Would you continue waiting just because the store was cool? Would you buy the product anyway, and figure your questions weren't important? No.

Lloyd-Martin, 2008

Flash can look appealing, but most search engines can't index Flash files or graphics, so all they see when they index a fancy Flash splash page is a site's title and meta tags (if they exist). With no more content to index, search engine spiders, hungry for site content and text, will simply leave the Flash site.

Submitting your site to the search engines

Once you have optimized your site, you need to submit it to the search engines. To make your job of submitting easier, you should prepare a text file with the following:

- your site's main URL;
- the URLs for other pages on your site that you will be submitting;
- your site's title;
- a short (10–20 words) description of your page/site content;
- a longer (30–50 words) description of your page/site content;
- name of person mailing the submission;
- e-mail address of submitter;
- address and contact details of your company.

Use target keywords as much as possible when creating your site descriptions. Be sure, however, not to overstuff with keywords. Once you have these elements ready, you are ready to submit to the search engines.

Here are some rules to follow:

- Do it once.

- Do it properly (be very thorough).

- Be brief.

- Be accurate.

- Be relevant.

- Be humble.

- Be patient.

In terms of the directories, you will need to select a category for your site. To do this, conduct a search for your keywords and then study the related categories. Look at the sites within these categories and choose that category which is the most closely related to your site's content.

For the directories, submit to Yahoo!, Open Directory, About.com/ Sprinks, AOL, Looksmart, MSN Live Search.

As for search engines, submit to Google, AltaVista, Ask, FAST/All the Web, HotBot, Lycos.

How to measure your results

Once your SEO campaign is implemented, you absolutely need to track your campaign and measure its success. There are a number of ways to do this:

- Track your site's search engine rankings.

- Track the amount of traffic your site is receiving.

- Track the number of returning visitors to your site.

- Track the number of sales/conversions your site receives.

- Track the link popularity of your site.

Remember that it is not just where you rank that is important. It's the quality of traffic your site receives and what you do with the traffic that count. Today it is widely understood that rankings are meaningless unless the traffic they bring in leads ultimately to sales.

It is better to have 20 visitors to your site, 15 of whom will purchase a product or service than to have 500, of whom 5 make a purchase.

Several variables should be examined on a regular basis in relation to metrics and conversion:

- Pathways through your site.

- The page from which most visitors click away from your site. (Is there a technical problem? Do you have links to an external site that is inducing clients to click away before buying? Is there something on this page that is encouraging visitors to leave?)

- Single access pages.

- Most visited page and top entry pages.

- Landing pages for pay-per-click campaign.

- Metric values that show a radical change from developing trends.

- Page refreshes.

- Where your site visitors are coming from.

- Search engine referrals.

- Search phrases.

With the advent of Web 2.0, the role of the search engine is changing. On the one hand, people are starting to find sites through other ways: feeds, blogs, podcasts, vlogs (video blogs) and other pathways. There is also the possibility of finding sites through word of mouth, traditional advertising, traditional media and links from other sites. Many of these alternative forms can be as effective as, if not more effective than, search engines. Search marketing needs to be complemented with other online and offline media.

Know when to stop

Finally, it's important to know when to stop. A few changes may be enough to achieve top rankings. But that's not enough for some people, who try endlessly to do better. Perhaps this time could be put to better use pursuing non-search engine methods.

Don't obsess over your ranking. Even if you follow every tip and find no improvement, you have still gained something. You will know that search engines are not the way you'll be attracting traffic. Concentrate your efforts elsewhere and don't waste your valuable time.

Summary

- Search engines lie at the heart of the internet. Thus, ignoring search engine optimization is a big mistake.
- If you have a great site and no one shows up, it won't be much of a party.
- Find a good SEO copywriter; he or she will be worth their weight in gold.
- Don't worry about keeping up with the algorithms; just remember to work on keyword prominence, keyword density and link popularity.
- Don't obsess over SEO. Fulfil the basics. Know when to stop.

7 The forgotten magic of article marketing

Using articles to establish yourself as a thought leader

Article marketing is the great forgotten voice of the new media.

As search engines continue to revise their algorithms and put more importance on content rather than design, article e-marketing moves to the forefront as an excellent internet marketing tool.

The concept is simple

The concept of article marketing is simple. You write articles for free and provide them to other websites, blogs and e-zines. Your payback? On each article, you include a short biography that links back to your site.

Article marketing can establish you as an online thought leader, increase your site traffic, provide you with leads and improve your search engine rankings. A PR, SEO and marketing aid all rolled into one.

Each article is your business partner

The best way to imagine how article marketing works is to consider each article that you write to be a business partner (Dean and

McCausey, 2008). These business partners are marketing your business 24 hours a day, seven days a week. They are busy getting your name exposed, establishing you as an expert and driving traffic to your site.

Writing articles for the web is one of the easiest and quickest ways to become recognized as an expert in your specialized field. You will enter into a virtuous cycle. If you produce and submit content-rich articles to various publishing sites, these will be picked up by other publishers and your content will be used on their websites. As more and more publishers use your articles, you get numerous quality inbound links and increased online exposure.

Article marketing benefits

What are the benefits of article marketing?

- Article marketing is long term. An article, once written, works for you for a long time.

- Article marketing costs next to nothing.

- Article marketing gives you targeted, free traffic.

- Article marketing provides you with high exposure both on- and offline. It can open doors to offline media like radio, television and the press.

- Article marketing allows you to get your articles published in newsletters and websites that often don't accept advertising. With article marketing, you can find yourself being endorsed by a big newsletter to which you wouldn't normally have access.

- Article marketing can brand you as an online thought leader very quickly. Once you establish yourself as an expert, people will be more open to network or create a joint venture with you.

- Article marketing allows you to gain the trust of your prospective clients before they even arrive at your website. Instead of arriving at your website cold, they arrive warmed up and open to your product offerings.

- Article marketing helps you improve your search engine rankings. For most search engines, incoming links show that a website has value and authority. The more incoming links you have, the more value your website has. You can beg for incoming links. You can pay for incoming links. Or you can write articles.

- Article marketing can benefit *anyone*. Whether you have an information site, a lead generation site, a direct sales business or a blog, you can enjoy increased traffic and higher SEO rankings through article marketing.

Before you write your first article

Before you write your first article, you need to set up your website and do keyword research.

First set up your website

You need to be sure that your website incorporates the following:

- A media or 'about us' page so that if a newspaper or magazine sees and likes your article, they will know how to contact you.
- An e-newsletter sign-up box so that you can stay in touch with the prospects who click onto your website.
- The best conversion rate possible. If you are currently getting a low conversion rate, you will need to tweak your website. It is essential that your website is capable of turning traffic into cash and be 'ready to sell'.

The key is keyword research

If you don't research good keywords, you are approaching your article marketing campaign blind.

Your goal is to get front-page rankings for both your website pages and the article directory pages which hold your articles.

Knowing your market and choosing good keywords are essential. If you target a keyword that has too much competition, your article will fail with the search engines. If you target a keyword with not enough search volume, your article will fail with the search engines. If you target a keyword that is irrelevant to your website's topic, your article will be useless and your visitors disappointed.

Keyword research for your articles is no different than research for your web page. The only difference is, generally, you'll be targeting keywords with a little less competition for your articles.

Find words with good search volume but little competition

Your primary goal should be finding keywords that have a lot of search volume but little competition, and are extremely relevant to the topic of the site your articles will promote. How do you do this?

Step one: use an accurate keyword research tool. Type in a term. You will see the search volume for that keyword phrase as well as the data for several related keywords.

Step two: since your website itself will be targeting the main keyword, you want to find related keywords with less search volume for your articles. However, don't forget that a keyword with low search volume can still be highly competitive (just as a high search volume keyword can be less competitive).

Step three: open Google and start searching. Plug in each of the related keywords you have found. Look at the quality of the pages in the top 10. Be sure to examine the page that is being linked to and *not* the site that the page belongs to. In other words, just because a page belongs to a high-ranking site doesn't necessarily mean that the page itself has much authority. When you examine each page, you need to look for the keyword density of the title, the Google page-rank indicator and the number of incoming links to the page.

The perfect keyword is one that gets a lot of search volume but has little or no competition.

So, what do you do with the keywords once you find them?

First of all, it is important to emphasize that you really shouldn't worry about keywords in your article body. If you can incorporate your keywords in there a few times, that is great. But you should concentrate on writing naturally and the finished product will be of a higher quality.

Keywords must be in your title

The keywords absolutely need to be included in your title. The article title is the single most important factor in getting your article found by both humans and search engines.

You want to include your main keyword in the first four words of the title. But once again, the keywords in the title should be there naturally. Don't overstuff.

Your title should stand out from the competition's

There is one other consideration with regards to the title. It is essential that your title is interesting as well. You need to be able to stand out from the competition.

There is a final use for your keywords. Many article directories will allow hyperlinks in the body of the article (from one to three hyperlinks). Convert your target keywords to hyperlinks. This will bring your website direct traffic through clicks and will help improve your site's search engine rankings for that keyword.

Finding subjects for your article

You should write articles that are related to the subject of your website. This is extremely important. As I mentioned earlier, your article is warming people up as potential customers. You have the unique opportunity to show prospects that you are an expert on your topic. So don't talk about one subject and then send them to a website which is about a completely different subject.

Stick to what you like and know. Your articles shouldn't be forced. If they are forced, the article won't be fun to read.

To collect ideas, you should start an ideas folder. Get ideas from many different sources. Look through your website.

Look through your blog entries.

Look at old papers or newsletters you have written.

Look at posts you've written on forums.

Look at e-mails you have written.

Writing the article

Once you have your idea, you are ready to put pen to paper. There are a host of devices you can use to start the creative juices flowing. The article can be in the form of a journal to a friend or customer. Or you can interview someone. What about starting the article with a poll or quiz? How-to articles are another option. And, finally, you can create an article series on any given subject.

Here are some tips for the article:

- Use simple terms, short sentences and clear explanations. Define highly technical words. Relate difficult ideas to life situations. Use images to help your readers visualize concepts. Remember, the main objective is that the reader understand your ideas – not that they have to struggle to navigate through them.

- Make sure your article can be easily scanned. Use bullet points, white blank spaces and do not appear too wordy. Equally, you need to break your articles into sections. An article that is composed of a couple of paragraphs will not perform as well as the exact same article broken down into easily digested segments.

- Use a conversational tone. Make it upbeat and interesting. Pretend you are talking directly to your readers.

- Make sure that your article is free of any errors: grammar and typos. You want to look your best; your article should represent you well. Proofread, proofread, proofread.

- Check your facts. This will help your reader trust you and follow your recommendations. Additionally, your articles may very well be used by other webmasters and they will want to be sure that they are factually correct. An article full of factual errors could easily ruin your online credibility.

- Don't make your article an advertisement or press release. The article body should *never* mention your service, product or website.

- Never write less than 300 words or more than 600. Always vary the length article by article. Remember, the goal is for people to click on your resource box. If they get bored wading through too much text, they will stop reading and never click on your website.

- Set a goal for how many articles you will write. Write at least two articles a month, preferably two a week. Never skimp on quality. It is better to have 50 good articles than 200 bad ones.

- Don't borrow ideas from other article writers. As an expert in your field, you shouldn't have problems creating articles uniquely designed for your target market.

- Ask for feedback from your readers.

- Make sure you know the guidelines of the directories when you submit your articles.

- Create content that is 100 per cent unique, making sure that the content does not get published anywhere else. Don't take content directly from your website and then submit it to the directories in article form. This will be viewed as duplicate content by the search engines and will disappoint your viewers who will click on your link only to find the exact same material on your website.

- Tease your reader with valuable information but don't tell them everything.

- Be specific. Keep your content focused on one central theme. Don't introduce unrelated topics in your articles.

- Use powerful language. Use the active voice to increase the power in all your articles. Never use the passive voice, as it will weaken your content.

- Direct your readers. Take charge and give them recommendations.

Don't forget the resource box!

Aside from your title, your resource box is the most important part of your article. Oddly enough, many people spend lots of time writing their articles and then barely pay attention to their resource box.

Your resource box is the place where you brand yourself. Remember that the article itself should be used for teaching and informing, not advertising. Do your selling in the resource box.

Remember, there are two goals for article marketing. One is to get incoming links. The second is to get visitors to click on your website. Without a good resource box, you will never attain this second objective.

Here is a list of essential items for your resource box:

- Your name (this should be the first thing in your resource box).

- Your website address in valid URL form (be careful there are no broken links). If your article is about a topic which is covered in one of the internal pages of your website, then use that link in your signature instead of your main URL. Don't put a full stop at the end of your link or you will end up with an error page.

- Your 'elevator pitch': a one- to three-sentence description of you and your company and what makes you unique.

- Your call to action: lead them to buy from you or visit your website.

You should avoid a listing of every website you own. Post only *one* URL that is directly related to your article topic. Equally, you should not include a listing of every accomplishment you've achieved to date. Keep your resource box simple and brief.

Your resource box should be no larger than 20 per cent of your total article size.

How to submit articles

After having written the article itself, it may seem tedious to then have to submit your work. However, this phase is crucial to the success of your article marketing programme.

There are services that will manually submit your articles for you. However, if you cannot afford them, then you must submit them yourself.

Do not compromise on this phase. It is critical to your success. Find at least twelve article directories. Then build from there. If you get to twenty directories, you are doing well.

In the past, search engine algorithms did not discriminate against mass submission services. This meant that the more article sites you could find to submit to, the better. A few of the more popular services are ArticleMarketer.com and iSnare.com. They are not effective any more.

Submit half of your articles to only the top few article directories:

- EzineArticles.com;
- ArticleDashboard.com;
- Buzzle.com;
- WebProNews (internet marketing related articles only);
- IdeaMarketers.com;
- ArticleAlley.com;
- ArticleCube.com.

Submit the other half to 40–60 of the best article directories you can find.

Submitting half of your articles to the top few sites means that those article pages, because they appear on a handful of quality sites, will continue to rank high with the search engines and bring in a constant flow of traffic directly through the article sites.

By submitting the other half of your articles to 40–60 of the best article directories, you will receive the initial flood of traffic, but it will slow down as the content is no longer unique. But your 'mass submission' is limited compared to article submissions services, and if the sites are quality, most of the pages will get indexed in the search engines, providing one-way links to your site. In the long run, those links will add up and increase your search engine exposure.

In addition, you can find authority sites in your niche. Many sites will publish articles submitted by others. Find a contact form or e-mail address and let them know that you produce quality articles that are very relevant to their website and that you would like to offer them your articles on a weekly or daily basis.

Getting your articles published on popular sites will provide you strong back links, a boost in site visitors and credibility. It can also provide more of an opportunity for your articles to get picked up by big e-zine and e-newsletter publishers.

Furthermore, seek out e-zines and e-newsletters in your niche.

Having just one article distributed to an e-newsletter or e-zine with a large circulation can literally convert to thousands of dollars overnight.

Social bookmarking can help

A final thought is about social bookmarking. Every time you submit an article, you need to social-bookmark it. Some of the most well-known social bookmarking sites are Reddit, Digg, Delicious and StumbleUpon. By social-bookmarking your articles, you will give them the potential to go viral.

A word about social bookmarking sites – one estimate says there are 15 billion discrete web pages (as opposed to websites). It is hard to make sense of it all. We can't possibly remember where we have been; we need to pluck out the best pages and save them for later.

The old way is to bookmark, ie add a page to the favourites on your web browser. It is a bit messy and the problem is that your favourites list remains tied to just one computer. Social bookmarking is the new alternative; instead of using your browser, you use a social book-marking website.

The basic idea is that you tag a site you like and place it at a social bookmarking site such as Delicious. When you tag a site, a window will open and ask you to put in additional information. You enter tags or key words so that you can remember what the page in question is about. With these tags, it will be much easier to find the site later – and it is a way to share your results with others. And that is the essence of social bookmarking sites – to share your favourite sites with others. Those looking for the same topics as you will look at other people's opinions on pages and it will help them in their search.

Finally, participation in larger social bookmarking networks like Digg and StumbleUpon can really help you get known. When a company gets an article, video or other content Dugg or StumbledUpon, huge numbers of visitors see the content. This has the potential to create an avalanche effect which will drive more and more traffic to your site.

You will need to track results

There are many ways to track your results. Here are a few:

- PageRank.net;
- Link popularity tool;
- Stats on article directories;
- Own website stats;
- Awstats analysis software;
- Google Analytics.

Always remember that every article you have out there will continue to bring in visitors. As article marketing guru and EzineArticles.com publisher Christopher Knight is reported as saying:

'Each article you submit should be thought of as an agent.' This is a great way to think of it, as each article is like an employee, out there to bring in viewers.

Spaulding, 2008

Summary

Here are the key points for article writing:

- Article marketing is a very powerful but often forgotten internet marketing tool.
- Article marketing can establish you as an online thought leader.
- Keyword research is essential for success.
- Your resource box – not your article – is your selling tool.
- Each article is your agent, living long after you have distributed it.

8 From Citizen Kane to citizen journalists

Let the power of blogs enhance your business performance

> Blogs help small businesses seem big and big businesses feel small.
>
> Weber, 2007

> If you don't talk with your employees and your customers in a way that lets them in on things, you're missing out on the game.
>
> Marc Gunther (article on CNN.com)

Perhaps the best known form of social media, blogs symbolize the new media and the changing terrain of the internet.

Companies who do not blog will be at a disadvantage.

Companies with blogs – and who do it right – will create superior customer and employee relationships.

Definition

'Blog' is short for weblog. A blog is an online diary with entries appearing in reverse chronological order. People share their thoughts, activities, reactions and opinions with each other on a blog. They write their ideas using posts, an article or comment written on the blog.

A blog tends to be the jurisdiction of one author. The author decides the scope and 'voice' of the blog. A blog contains stories, links and any other information that the author deems interesting.

A blogger is like a DJ on a radio show. He chooses stories or links like a DJ chooses songs. Audiences not only 'tune in' to his show, but also contribute to it by posting comments.

Blogs take as many forms as there are individuals. They range from free-form exercises in self-expression to tight themes built on passions or favourite interests.

A blog is anything the author wants it to be.

How blogs differ from a Web 1.0 world

Web 1.0 is static and changes little. It is like a library which contains a collection of reference documents you read at leisure. Blogs represent the exact opposite. As posts and links are added, blogs constantly change.

A blog is not a blog without links

Bloggers look at each other's blogs. When they read something that piques their interest, they link to it and comment on it. Therefore, when you arrive at one blog, it will have links connecting you to other blogs. Blogs are all about links.

There is a special kind of blog link called a permalink. Short for 'permanent link', this is a URL that links to a specific news story or web posting. A permalink gives a specific web address to each posting which allows blog entries to be linked to other websites or bookmarked by visitors.

Why is this important? Even if a blog posting is outdated and has been moved from the home page to archives, it will still remain accessible through the permalink. The use of permalinks to define the location of each posting prevents blog entries from fading into oblivion.

The permalink transformed blogs from an an easy publishing idea into a 'conversational mess of overlapping communities'. The permalink built solid bridges between blogs.

A trackback is another method that helps links. It lets a blogger know when another blogger has commented upon one of his posts. He can then respond through a reciprocal link or by adding a comment.

The blogosphere is an infinite global conversation

The blogosphere is the sum of all these cross-linked blogs and constitutes a global conversation. The thread from blog to blog is quite literally infinite. If you tracked millions of blogs simultaneously, you could create a heat map showing the thoughts and conversations of people.

People call the blogosphere the 'live web'. And links are the DNA of the live web.

There are a lot of micro-communities within the blogosphere

There is not one big mammoth blogosphere. There are hundreds of thousands of little networks that revolve around specific topics. In other words, a lot of little micro-communities. Niche after niche after niche. This is why the blogosphere is so good at chasing after what Chris Anderson has called the Long Tail. The Long Tail describes the niche strategy of businesses that sell a large number of unique items in relatively small quantities.

Blogs are open to the world

E-mail is also an ongoing conversation, with billions of conversations occurring over the past 10 years. However, there is an important difference between e-mail and blogs. One is private and the other is public. Blogs are open to the world: anyone can read them, anyone can contribute to them.

The blog conversation, unlike e-mail or even professional mass media, is open to the public from the beginning. A professional researches, writes and edits stories in private. He guards his 'scoop' closely until the story is released to the public. Blogs are much more democratic and less elitist.

There are no editorial constraints

Bloggers are citizen journalists. But unlike ordinary journalists, bloggers write with no editorial constraints. If they can get their ideas in front of a large enough audience, they potentially exercise a lot of power. Some can make or break personal, product or corporate reputations.

Blogs blur mainstream definitions

Blogs and mainstream sites are blurring together. Many sites are blogs but readers just aren't aware of this. Blog posts mingle with publications of all sizes, both on- and offline. Blogs bear testimony to the fact that traditional media are now being eroded by the 'people's voice'.

With blogs, the divide between the public and publishing evaporates. The public *is* the publisher. Mass media is replaced (at least theoretically) by the media of the masses.

Traditional media lose control

With the advent of the blog, companies who were used to controlling their message began to lose control of it. Since the invention of the printing press, a chosen few controlled the information. Professional journalists held story secrets close to their hearts. Big companies massaged their messages until they were ready to be introduced to highly defined target audiences. This was mass media, a closed, jealously guarded system.

Blogs turn this world upside down. Blogs dispense with the need for a printing press, an editorial board or an advertising agency. Anyone with a computer and internet connection becomes a publisher with the snap of a finger. It is an open, democratic process – diametrically opposed to the closed, elitist one of traditional communication.

Blogs bestow power

Blogs represent power. No one need any longer be beholden to professional media. And if you are clever and master the art of blogging, you can talk persuasively to a huge audience and wield great power.

More than any other social media tool, blogs are the most difficult to avoid. They have become part of the fabric. Nowadays it is sometimes difficult to tell whether you are reading a blog or a website; the borders between the two remain blurred.

As Clay Shirky, a web expert at New York University, says, it's 'an absorption process where the thing doing the absorbing changes'. Mainstream media refer to blog information. And people increasingly look to blogs to give them timely, expert advice and information.

Blogs publish stories just like 'regular' newspapers, radio and television stations. Mainstream media acknowledges this contribution more and more. At the White House, bloggers intermingle with nationally known network reporters.

Blog reporters have great value. During the Asian tsunami, thousands posted pictures, articles and video footage about the disaster. And many reported much more quickly than the traditional press.

It is hard to say that one blog – or even several blogs – can compete with mainstream media. But it is fair to say that the blogosphere as a whole competes with mainstream media.

The blogosphere collectively has a strength which is difficult to ignore.

Twitter is the new It girl of blogging

Microblogging stands tall as the new It girl of blogging. The hyperconnected are obsessed by Twitter.com. Twitter is a microblogging device where you can blog in 140 characters or less. It is perfect for the mobile age because you can Twitter through your mobile phone.

Search engines love blogs

Search engines love blogs because they love fresh content. Search engine spiders visit blogs often, resulting in much better search engine rankings. Because search engines use link structures to predict useful pages, blogs – with their prolific links – enjoy a disproportionate role in directing search engine results.

Why do people get involved with blogs?

Figure 8.1 breaks down the activities people engage in when blogging.

What motivates people to start and maintain a blog? A lot of people seek visibility or want to be recognized as an expert or an authority. Others look to blogs to advance their career, connect with others, influence markets or simply make them feel good.

In other words, the blog machine operates on people's passion to communicate rather than cash. Any power a blog might have must be measured in terms of influence rather than in terms of money.

This situation could change as mass media come to grips with a splintering audience. While advertisers grow desperate to tap into niches, blogs could prove to be a perfect vehicle to help them.

Compare a blog with regular websites

One way to better understand a blog is to compare it with 'normal' websites.

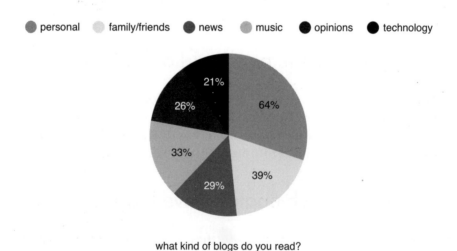

what kind of blogs do you read?

Figure 8.1 People's favourite blog subjects

Normal websites have a home page and links to a lot of sub-pages. Traditional websites follow more or less the same format whether they have 5, 10 or 1,000 pages.

A large majority of websites act as online brochures. As a calling card, they describe an individual or a company and are static and unchanging in nature.

By comparison, a blog, in its sheer simplicity, is ever-changing.

A basic blog can be set up in a matter of minutes. Simple web-based tools like WordPress, Blogger, Xanga, TypePad and LiveJournal help you to create a basic blog. If you want additional features, you will usually need to pay an additional fee.

A blog has a main page. That's all. On the main page, you will find a set of entries. Each entry is a little text blurb that will have links in it which will go to other news sites or news stories, etc.

On that main page, the entries are organized in reverse chronological order. You see the most recent entry first. Whenever the author of the blog adds a new entry, it will go to the top and will push all the older entries down.

In addition, blogs have a right sidebar which contains permanent links to other sites and stories.

The RSS factor again

RSS (Real Simple Syndication) feeds are another very important blog feature. People sign up to your RSS feed. When you post an article on your blog, those people will immediately receive information about your post. They can either read the post on your blog or they will read it with their RSS reader or aggregator. These are personalized web pages which bring together the music, video and news that the user has signed up for.

Aggregators are powerhouses in their own right. Google Reader is an example of one such aggregator – a staple for many in the blogging community.

Aggregators constitute a potential revolution on the internet. They discourage surfing through search engines which, to date, has been the way that people have found information on the internet. Users instead wait for interesting items to show up on their page or in their e-mail box.

Aggregators also help to increase the prestige of blog material. When you begin to receive information through your aggregator, you will soon see that blog posts stand side-by-side with news blurbs from prestigious organizations like Associated Press and the New York Times.

We're getting bloggier

'Blogs are what's causing the web to grow', says Jason Goldman, Project Manager at Google Blog, the world's biggest service to set people up as bloggers (quoted by Stephen Baker and Heather Green in their article published on BusinessWeek.com).

According to Wikipedia, as of June 2008 the Technorati blog search engine indexes 112 million blogs with 120,000 new ones coming up each day. However, it is important to point out that only 11 per cent of those blogs were posted within the preceding two months. So the active blog universe probably totals around 13 million blogs.

Gartner, the technology research company, believes that the number of blogs has levelled out at 100 million. According to Daryl Plummer, a Gartner analyst, most people who have wanted to start a blog have already done so. Gartner also claims that more than 200 million people have stopped writing their blogs.

After an average of three months, many bloggers get bored with the idea and move on to the next shiny object (Weber, 2007). 'A lot of people have been in and out of this thing', says Plummer. 'Everyone thinks they have something to say until they're put on stage and asked to say it.' The result is a lot of dead blogs that fall by the wayside after a few months.

Among the reasons why people lose interest in blogs is the fact that they require a lot of writing – something many people are not very good at. Second, blogs require a huge time commitment (Solis and Livingston, 2007). According to many blog experts, you need to be prepared to put in at least 8–10 hours a week on your blog. If you are working with an agency, plan on a 30–40-hours-a-month retainer. Many corporate blogs have started out with a big bang and then over a period of a few years slowed down to a trickle.

Blogging is demanding, and many give up

Blogs have their share of critics. As someone wryly commented, the average blog has the lifespan of a fruit fly. (Real detractors went on to sardonically comment that the average blog has the intelligence of a fruit fly: 'Blog statistics and demographics', published on Caslon.com.au.)

Humour aside, the reality is that blogging is demanding – particularly if you are already running a business. As John Dragoon, Chief Marketing Officer of Novell, Inc, explains, 'It's far easier to start a blog than to keep one going. Blogging – in addition to the demands of running a business – is no easy task' (quoted by Jackie Noblett in article published on the Boston Business Journal website).

When companies first rushed to the new medium, many didn't understand the nature of the blogosphere and hadn't even identified their target audience.

Consistency is key

Companies often wonder how blogs fit into their corporate philosophy and are wondering how to keep a blog relevant and timely. But consistency is key.

'If the goal is to get people to come back, then you really need to be doing it on a regular basis. Several days a week is a minimum; anything less than that is not really a blog', says Dan Kennedy, Assistant Professor of Journalism at Northeastern University and author of the popular Media Nation blog.

Nevertheless, Dragoon is positive and feels that blogging allows an opportunity for transparency which is often lacking in public companies. 'I personally enjoy blogging and feel it is well within my scope to use my experiences and be a part of the social medium spectrum', he says. 'I think it has humanized Novell' (Noblett; see above).

While bloggers drop out, the community who reads blogs continues to grow. The fact that there are more readers is definitely good news for the remaining blogs. If they play their cards right, they can potentially wield heavy influence.

Blogging benefits

Blogging benefits companies in many ways:

- You can be viewed as a thought leader, shedding insight onto your company's philosophy and personality.

- You can position yourself as an expert.

- You can increase your credibility.

- You can 'talk' with your customer, receiving feedback about your products, service and company. 'I'm amazed people don't get it yet', says Jeff Weiner, Yahoo!'s senior vice-president who heads up search. 'Never in the history of market research has there been a tool like this' (Baker and Green; see above).

- You can 'talk' with your employee, creating a more positive working environment.

- You can use it as an instant communication vehicle in which customers can receive product updates and other news through RSS feeds (BusinessBlogMarketing.com).

Successful blogging examples

Probably the most famous example of successful corporate blogging is Sun Microsystems. Jonathan Schwartz, CEO, explains:

> Leadership is all about communications, it's what leaders do. Almost by definition, your set of responsibilities comes down to who you pick to work for you, how much budget you give them, and then what do you say all day long when you are trying to motivate change and drive people forward. So blogging is a tool that, especially for leaders, is critical to amplify your communications.
>
> Quoted in Weber, 2007

For Schwartz, blogging is 'living the brand' and gives an authentic voice to an organization. He emphasizes that an insincere voice will not work. And silence is even worse. 'In a vacuum, somebody else will be speaking on your behalf about your company, about your brands, about your executives or about your employees' (Weber, 2007).

When Schwartz decided that any Sun Microsystems employee could have a blog, his legal team was horrified. His public relations department panicked. Carte blanche blogging essentially meant anyone in the company could issue a press release. But the company has avoided any problems by giving out simple, general guidelines which have been respected: 'Don't do anything stupid... Write about something you know about... Make it interesting.'

The Sun Microsystems example illustrates that you need confidence to give up control. Through its blog (and, of course, other measures), Sun has begun to rebuild its stature as a competitive force in the IT industry (Weber, 2007).

General Motors is another leading company in blog communications. The GM blog is called FastLane (see Figure 8.2). It was launched by Vice-Chairman Bob Lutz, who also enlists the help of other senior executives at GM. The blog is sometimes used to steer past his own PR department and the mainstream press.

FastLane does not represent a revolution. But it is undoubtedly an important communications tool for the company.

An example of a group blog is Poliblog, Verizon's blog in which executives discuss technology and telecommunication policy.

Wells Fargo hosts a blog called Guided by History (Figure 8.3), which is all about natural disasters and addresses questions like 'How do you prepare for drought?'.

As we have seen with Sun Microsystems, technology companies have led the way in business blogging. IBM and Microsoft have thousands of bloggers, many of whom write for small, specialized audiences. Robert Scoble of Microsoft has become a celebrity and gone on

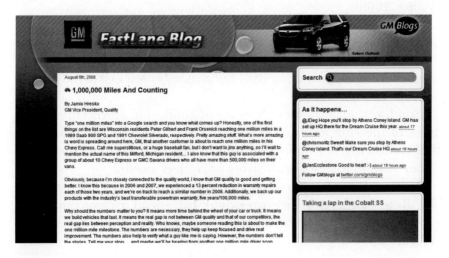

Figure 8.2   GM's FastLane blog

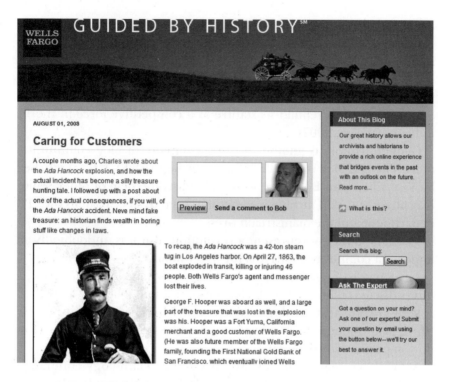

Figure 8.3   Wells Fargo's Guided by History blog

to write a popular book about blogging called *Naked Conversations* (Wiley, 2006).

According to *The Economist*, Scoble 'has succeeded where small armies of more conventional public-relations types have been failing abjectly for years; he has made Microsoft, with its history of monopolistic bullying, appear marginally but noticeably less evil to the outside world.'

Southwest Airlines' blog, Nuts about Southwest, affirms the quirkiness of the company culture (Figure 8.4). It successfully balances between being fun and being informational. It elicits participation from its employees while satisfying its readers' needs.

McDonald's blog is called Open for Discussion and is written by Bob Langert, a vice-president for social responsibility. It covers topics ranging from obesity to negotiating with Greenpeace (Figure 8.5).

Figure 8.4   Southwest Airlines' Nuts about Southwest blog

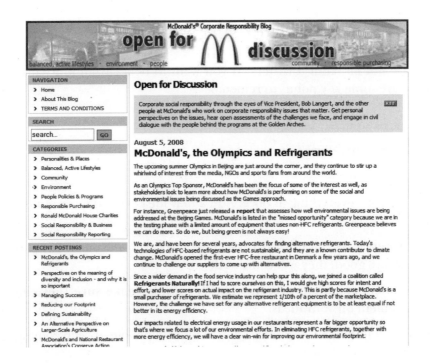

Figure 8.5   McDonald's blog

Then there are the failures

Then there are the abject failures: for example, Wal-Mart's blog called Wal-Marting Across America. The blog was ostensibly written by a man and a woman travelling across the country in an RV and staying in Wal-Mart parking lots at night. But the venture turned out to be a farce; it was not the work of two objective customers but instead the product of Wal-Mart's public relations firm, Edelman. Needless to say, an uproar ensued. Despite an apology from Edelman's president, the public was unforgiving. It was too little, too late.

What do you need to know if you want to effectively communicate with your blog?

According to Debbie Weil, author of *The Corporate Blogging Book* (Penguin, 2006), you must be open, honest and authentic. You must write with a human voice and post often. Anything that feels artificial or controlled just won't work.

Make sure you have a robust and constructive conversation with your readers through the comment section.

Writing hints for successful blogging

We are not all natural writers. If you want to be a citizen journalist, there are some key points to remember:

- Use headlines. Headlines engage busy readers.

- Write short. Write fast.

- Be exciting.

- Don't say everything at once. Add a new idea every day, creating a thesis over time.

- Include links. It's OK to distract people away from your writing. If you are good, they will come back.

- Readers are interested in what *they* think. Make sure they can comment on your ideas.

- Forget gimmicks. Gimmicks don't motivate people to keep coming back to your blog.

- Use lists. People love lists.

- Write on a regular basis.

- Not writing is bad.

- Trying to be perfect every time you write is even worse.

The problem with blogs

It's important to talk about the negative side of blogs.

The first problem which strikes terror in the heart of most CEOs is the idea that blogs encourage negative comments about people, products or the company itself.

No one likes to be criticized. And it's particularly hard to face when we were the ones who actually wrote the materials. One way of guarding against negative comments is to review comments before they are published. Some see this as 'cheating', since part of the blog philosophy is to be open and transparent – even to the negative comments.

A second issue which is almost as daunting is the idea of loss of control. Blogs just cannot be fully controlled. For companies who are used to top-down, controlled communication, this creates a lot of discomfort. It feels too risky. But if people are not talking with you, they will talk about you. At the end of the day, it is better to enter into the dialogue and at least tell your side of the story.

A third issue reigns as the biggest. Letting your blog slide. Neglecting it. The amount of time and resources a blog requires should not be underestimated.

Not fully understanding the blogosphere culture can trip companies up. Make sure you take time to understand the type of language and tone of voice that are used in your corner of the blogosphere. Engage with the blogosphere as an individual before you actually launch your corporate blog.

Employees who are unprepared to be bloggers can cause you problems. If you have staff who don't understand your corporate culture but are still allowed to represent your company on a blog, you are in for trouble. Train your staff and give them guidelines. Tim Bray, Director of Web Technologies at Sun Microsystems, says he has 4,000 bloggers at Sun. This represents around 10 per cent of the workforce. According to Bray, there have been no problems with their blogs.

Another very small risk is the violation of privacy and trade secrets as well as the negative impact on share prices.

You could be sued for defamation. Retain documents in case there is a lawsuit.

Another risk is that you have no clear objectives. Sometimes you can get swept up into your blog without really thinking through what you want to do. A business blog can be started for any number of reasons: increased search engine visibility, improved customer communication or PR-building thought leadership.

Another problem is if you don't have enough resources. Blogs take loads of thought, time and manpower. If done well, however, they're worth it: a successful blog puts a personality on an anonymous corporation.

Another issue can be insufficient content. There are many ways to generate content. You can run polls, review blogs, cover conferences, write about common consumer issues, invite guests to post, review books, list resources and interview well-known people.

Prohibiting comments can be problematic. Many business blogs prohibit comments; they don't like them, they are afraid of them. At the end of the day, a blog that doesn't take comments is not really a blog. Comments are good. Comments add richness to your blog. Feedback of any kind generates interest and conversation.

You need to understand the blogosphere culture. As with any community there are social norms. If these are ignored, the blogosphere will let you know with a slap on the hand. Possible negative effects can be significant. You need to be honest, transparent and authentic.

Promoting your blog

In order for your company blog to work, you must promote it well. Here are some of the things to think about when you set out to market your blog:

- Create a marketing plan.
- Enrol your blog in the blog search engines.
- Enrol your blog's RSS in RSS search engines.

- Tell your customers about your blog.

- Offer coupons or specials at least two to three times a month.

- Seek out bloggers who are blogging about your topics. Blog search engines like Technorati will help you find bloggers specific to your industry. Once you find a list of relevant bloggers, write about their blogs on your blog. Then ask these bloggers to review your blog. If they give you a positive review, this will help you add a good quality link.

- Publish periodic podcasts.

- Train your employees about your blog so they can help promote it.

Looking at a blog's ROI

Many companies seek to quantify and measure their blog to ensure that it is worth the resources invested in it. Here are a few ways to track the ROI of your blog:

- Remember that the blog will give you a deeper understanding of your consumer, which is worth its weight in gold.

- Use FeedBurner software to manage RSS feeds and track subscriber usage.

- Add online tracking software (eg Urchin, Webtrend), which will track unique visitors, page views and referrals.

- Track your blog by phone to understand what people ask after they review your blog.

What is the ultimate measure of success? This is what is so difficult for us to get our heads around. The ultimate measure of success is not a finished product. The winners are those who have the very best conversations. And how do you judge that?

What is the reality of blogs?

Blog readership is high. Of all the social media tools, blogs are the most mature (see Table 8.1 and Figure 8.6).

Table 8.1 Blog readership is growing around the world

	Sep 06 (%)	June 07 (%)	Mar 08 (%)
Global	54	66	73
Australia	21	55	62
China	58	85	88
France	75	77	78
Germany	20	15	55
Italy	79	76	79
Russia	73	72	71
South Korea	72	91	92
Spain	70	72	78
UK	38	54	66
USA	62	61	60

Source: Universal McCann

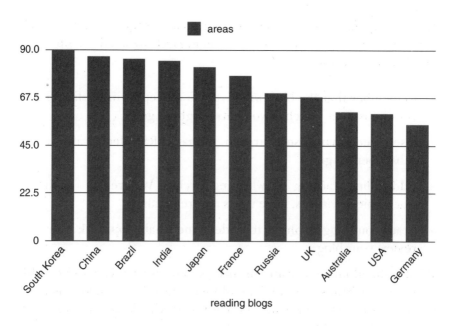

Figure 8.6 South Korea leads the world in blog readership

As is typical in social media, more people consume blogs than actually start their own. Having said that, Asia is a front-runner in the creation of blogs, with very heavy participation (Figure 8.7).

The important conclusion of the charts is that blogs are extremely popular with citizen journalists but have yet to really catch on in the corporate world.

A recent survey of the Fortune 500 notes that only 52 companies blog.

According to Steve Rubel, Senior Vice-President, Director of Insights, for Edelman Digital, blogs are probably less important for companies than people once thought they might be. Companies like that they can contact niche audiences through blogs. On the other hand, a lot of companies feel uncomfortable with the open, transparent communications that blogs require. Blogs, often viewed as personal, social and irreverent, are viewed with suspicion by conservative corporations.

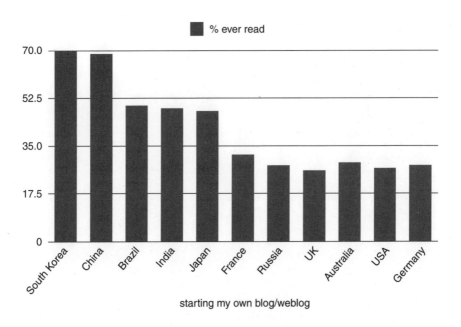

Figure 8.7   There are a log more blog readers than blog owners

Summary

- Blogs are the most mature social media tool.
- Blogs are beginning to blur with mainstream media.
- An authentic online voice is key.
- Be consistent; don't start out with a bang and end with a whimper.
- Corporations are way behind the citizen journalist in picking up the blog baton.

9 Podcasting – a toddler with a big future

Using podcast basics to help cement customer loyalty

> Podcasting is just a toddler... The toddler is extremely healthy and will be an extremely powerful figure.
>
> Paul Colligan, author of *The Business Podcasting Bible*, quoted in podcast by Marcus Chan

> Podcasting lets people sing to each other again.
>
> Dave Winer in article published on Scripting News website

Just imagine

Imagine you could talk to a highly targeted, tight-knit audience eager to know all about your market, your company and your products. What if they wanted to hear from you on a daily – or a weekly – basis? And what if you could create exciting value-laden content in a new format that held their attention each time? No more spam. No more nuisance. Only a great experience for you and your consumer alike.

Sound too good to be true?

A force of the future

Welcome to the exciting world of podcasting. This is a force to be reckoned with in the Web 2.0 world. Only a small percentage of people use podcasting on a regular basis right now. But don't underestimate the future potential power of podcasting.

Podcasting's technical components were available by 2001 and started showing up on well-known websites in 2003. Podcasting was named the word of the year by the editors of the *New Oxford American Dictionary* in 2005 (Weber, 2007).

eMarketer estimates that the total US podcast audience reached 18.5 million in 2007. That number should soar to 28 million in 2008 and increase by 251 per cent to 65 million in 2012. Even more surprising is that 25 million of those 65 million will be 'active' users who tune in at least once a week (see Figure 9.1).

Podcasts are also grabbing a piece of the multibillion-dollar online advertising pie. According to eMarketer, US advertisers spent $80 million in 2006 and $165 million in 2007. They also estimate the number will rise to $435 million in 2012.

And while more than one in five Americans have watched or listened to downloadable media (Figure 9.2)...

... it appears that the US trails behind other parts of the world; podcasting has caught on like wildfire in parts of Asia and Brazil (see Figure 9.3).

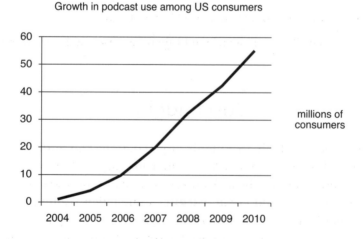

Figure 9.1 Podcasts are growing exponentially

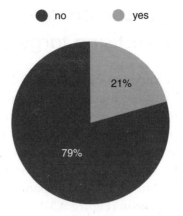

more than one in five Americans have watched
or listened to downloadable media

Figure 9.2 Over a fifth of Americans have watched/listened to downloadable media

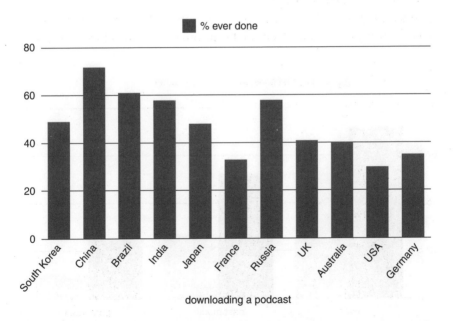

Figure 9.3 The US trails behind other parts of the world in podcasting

Podcast consumers are attractive advertising targets

Podcast consumers are very attractive as advertising targets. They are more likely to have a college degree and live in a household earning more than $75,000 per year. Americans who have watched or listened to podcasts shop more frequently online and spend more money online than other Americans (Figure 9.4).

Having said that, this is a group that resists online advertising. They are more likely to lock out pop-up ads, spam, and to use non-traditional means to view television (Figure 9.5).

Podcast consumers also spend more time on the internet every day than the average American.

A definition of podcasting

So what is podcasting exactly?

Podcasting, as a word, combines iPod and broadcasting. It refers to audio files available online that can be automatically downloaded so users

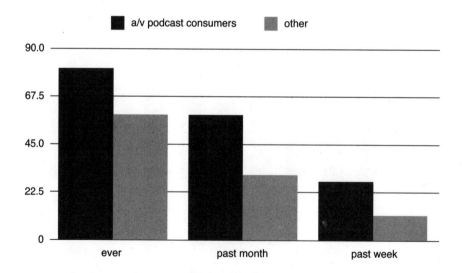

Figure 9.4   The US podcast consumer is an active online purchaser

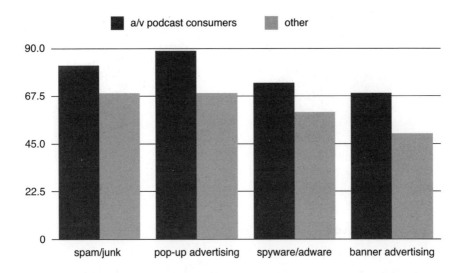

Figure 9.5 However, the US podcast consumer doesn't like unwelcome online advertising

can listen to them whenever and wherever they want. But podcasting doesn't require an iPod. You can use any portable media player or your computer to listen to your podcasts. The reality is that over 70 per cent of people download their media (audio and video) directly onto their computers and never use portable devices at all (Figure 9.6).

Wikipedia offers a complete definition of podcasting:

> Podcasting is a way of publishing files to a website that allows users to subscribe to the site and receive new files as they are posted. Most podcasts are spoken-word audio created by individuals, often on a particular theme such as technology or movies. Because new files are downloaded automatically by subscribers, podcasting allows individuals to have a self-published, syndicated radio show.

Podcasting blends the freedom of blogging with the technology of the MP3 player. With blogging, anyone with a computer can become a reporter. With podcasting, anyone with a computer can become a DJ, talk-show host or recording artist.

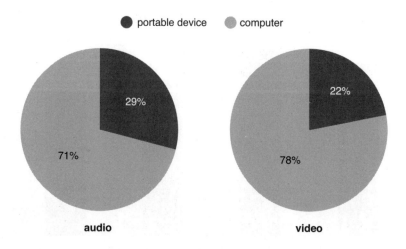

Figure 9.6 Most people listen to or watch downloadable media on their computer

Choosing when and where we listen to content

The beauty of podcasting is that you can decide exactly what content you want to receive. You download a podcast on demand or subscribe via an RSS feed which then automatically downloads the podcast to your computer. Through the RSS feed, you are automatically updated whenever a new podcast show is added.

Not unlike television services like TiVo and Sky+, podcasting then allows you to 'timeshift'. You don't have to listen to your podcast at a specified time. You can choose when and where to listen to it.

Both audio and video podcasting transform the broadcasting world. Instead of living in a world where pre-packaged content is pushed at us at specified times, we now live in a world where we can decide *what* we want to listen to *whenever* and *wherever* we wish.

Podcasting is a great equalizer. As a listener, you can consume whatever you want, whenever you want, wherever you want. As a content provider, anyone can create anything. Through podcasting, consumers become producers and enter actively into conversations they were never privy to before.

Simply put, podcasts are a flexible, novel way to promote your world – whether you are an individual or a small or large company.

Podcasting step by step

Podcasting is easy.

First step is to define your target audience and what you want to say to them.

Second, you record the audio on the web via desktop software, or over the telephone or with an external recorder.

The next optional steps include editing, adding music and creating text show notes based on the audio content.

Third, you convert your audio files to MP3 format.

Fourth, the converted audio files should be placed on the hosting server via file transfer protocol (FTP) or a web upload.

Finally, you publish your show and make it available to listeners, using blogging software or software on your web host.

How to find podcasts

You can find podcasts at many directories. Some of the most popular are iPodder.org, PodcastAlley (Figure 9.7), Podcasting News, Podshow, Podcast.net, the Podcast Directory and Podcast Pickle (Figure 9.8).

Moving beyond text

The internet is based on text. Search engines troll the web for text-based keywords. Consumers scan text to understand the meaning of a site. Even with this text bias, the internet is evolving to a world of pictures, sounds and motion. Even the most inexperienced computer novice designs his MySpace page full of animation, videos and songs.

But these new internet dimensions are not just fun and games. Podcasting, in particular, provides marketers with an excellent new way to inform and engage their prospects.

Many people retain information better when they hear it rather than read it. Audio can inject personality into your website in a way that text and graphics can't. Audio is convenient. Those who want to

Figure 9.7 Podcast Alley is a directory where you can find all kinds of podcasts

multitask can listen to audio while doing something else. Using audio can separate you from the competition. Many sites do not utilize audio. If you do, people will be attracted to your site versus the competition's.

Podcasts offer powerful communication possibilities

Podcast topics range from accounting to technology, community and politics, distance learning and sports. Whether you are an individual, a small company or a big multinational, podcasting offers infinite and powerful communication possibilities. Here are some of them:

Figure 9.8 On the Podcast Pickle website, you can find hundreds of different podcasts

- An internet radio show or talk show which contains rich content specifically designed for your target market.

- Distribution of class lessons.

- Conference meeting alerts and updates.

- Public safety messages.

- A teleclass series in which you interview experts giving tips to your target market.

- A 'day in the life' tour of someone in your company.

- An insider video on how you make products or produce services.

- A company update.

- Product updates or announcements.

- A thought-leadership position piece which discusses industry trends.

- Interviews with people in your industry or organization.

- Educational podcasts to give detailed information within the industry.

Podcasting speaks directly to communities of passion

Fred Greene of Smarter Podcasts talks about how podcasts talk directly to 'communities of passion' (reported in podcast by Cooligan and Greene). This phrase describes groups of enthusiasts who share keen interests. The examples are as varied as there are interests: skateboarders, skiers, gardeners, surfers, bicyclists, amateur photographers. If you happen to retail a 'passionate' product, podcasting marketing will deliver extremely positive results.

Edwin Watts Golf is a good example of how to use podcasting. Edwin Watts Golf signed up to podcast with the understanding they would not sell anything. Instead, they would contribute to the podcast's content. By doing this, they hoped to position themselves as a thought leader for golf. Their portion of the podcast answered submitted questions and covered the newest developments and techniques in golf.

Several listeners emailed Edwin Watts Golf stating they would make all their golf purchases from them simply because of the value they provided with their weekly podcasts. The podcast currently ranks at the top of YouTube sports categories (Cooligan and Greene podcast; see above).

The moral of the story? If you market to a community of passionate users, podcasting is a means to make them passionate about you as well.

Podcasts greatly benefit corporations large and small

The valuable benefits are many:

- Podcasts position you as a thought leader. This will not only increase customer satisfaction but help you acquire new clients.

- Podcasting defines your personality and image.

- Podcasting increases customer satisfaction.

- Podcasting helps you acquire new clients.

- Podcasts allow you to leverage a highly targeted, high-value listener. In this way, podcasting is 'narrowcasting' versus 'broadcasting'.

- Podcasting will make a big impact on your marketing mix.

- Your podcast audience bestows on you a direct, regular communication line to your target market, by saying 'I want to listen to you and your content' on a regular basis.

- Podcasting maximizes business intimacy.

- Podcasting boosts the bottom line.

How to create podcast content

Here are some rules you might want to keep in mind when you make your podcast:

- Keep your podcast short (7–20 minutes).

- Prepare. Don't stray. Keep the message clear and straightforward.

- Make sure your podcast is well produced, with high audio quality. Make it as professional as possible. Don't forget you are competing with the likes of US National Public Radio and the BBC.

- Don't sell in your podcast. People are looking for information, not an ad.

- Be thought-provoking and proactive.

- Keep your podcasting engaging and conversational.

- Know your target audience. Make sure to create a message that is relevant to them. Create loyal subscribers.

- Be organized.

- Edit for content, quality and length.

- Deliver engaging content that your listener can't get anywhere else.

- Provide show notes so that your listener can review the show's content.

- Tag your podcast so it can be easily found by podcasting software and directories.

- Ensure the RSS feed is valid and in compliance with the 2.0 standard.

- Submit your podcast to the popular directories.

- Consider having a co-host.

- Avoid a delivery that sounds like you are reading from a script.

- Avoid infrequent broadcasts. Continuity is important.

- Reformat existing format (webinars/teleseminars) or read previously written articles.

Podcasts are good for B2B...

Podcasts can be used in B2B as well. Using podcasts, you can generate more leads and nurture future customers. Buyers want to feel you understand them. They want to know the people who run the company. And they want you to be able to provide high-quality, thought-leading content. Podcasts provide all of these.

... as well as for internal audiences

Businesses can also use this technology both externally and internally as a communication medium to keep local, virtual and worldwide groups of clients or employees informed. This could be used for sales meetings for companies that have employees in worldwide locations. It is also an effective medium for distance learning, or for helping to get the entire team 'on message' on any specific topic.

But the best piece of advice about podcasting is that you will never truly understand podcasts until you start consuming them yourself.

Summary

- While podcasting is not widely used yet, it will be a force to be reckoned with in the future.
- Podcasts give you a chance to talk to a highly targeted audience on a consistent basis.
- Podcasts talk to communities of passion.
- Podcasts are turning the rules of broadcast upside down as we choose when, where and what we listen to.
- Podcasting positions you as a thought leader.

10 Social networking will be like air

Getting a grasp on the unavoidable, enhancing presence of social networks on the web

Some people predict that in 5–10 years social networking will be 'like air' (Li, 2008).

Some people argue that the internet will ultimately have more impact than television, radio or any other medium in the history of mankind. Social networks are at the centre of that revolution. They will prove to be the most powerful tool for both the social and the business side of online marketing.

The big names – names like MySpace, Facebook, Flickr, YouTube and LinkedIn – are just the tip of the iceberg.

New social networking sites are appearing all the time.

And many 'regular' sites are building some sort of social networking into their architecture. Sites like Amazon, eBay, AOL, Yahoo! and MSN all have social networking components.

Amazon is a good example. From its inception, the site's architecture was built around the concept of community. Amazon is far from just being an online retailer that sells books. It is a place where people are invited in to get to know the site, the other visitors and to join in the conversation. Amazon solicits your opinion and participation with everything it does.

Already, it feels like social networking is 'like air' (Li, 2008).

Description of a social network

What is a social network?

The concept of social networking has been around forever. A social network is simply a structure which maps out the relationships between individuals. One way or another, we all belong to one giant social network. Equally, we also belong to smaller, tighter networks defined by family, friends, the workplace, school and hobbies.

Take out a paper and pencil. Try to map out all the people to whom you're connected. Then try to map out all the people to whom *they* are connected. This is not an easy task.

The core idea of social networking is that you expand the number of people you know by meeting your friends' friends, their friends' friends, etc.

Social networking sites are powerful because they make invisible social networks visible. With pictures and links we can visually see who our friends are, who our friends' friends are and so on (Figure 10.1).

Social networking sites usually share one basic feature: the ability to create and share a personal profile. Profile pages normally include general personal information: a photo, a place to list favourite movies, TV shows, bands, books and websites.

Using the personal profile as a base, the social network then allows you to find and make friends with other people on the site. Each online social network has different rules. For example, MySpace is considered one of the most open. Facebook tends to be more exclusive and group-oriented. LinkedIn allows you to search every site member, although the full profile of someone is only available when that person has accepted your invitation to join your network.

What do people do on social networking sites? According to a Universal McCann study, the activities range from uploading photos and videos to listening to music, writing blogs and dating. The biggest activity by far is messaging friends (see Figure 10.2).

Millions flock to social networking sites

The seduction of social networking sites is irresistible to millions of people. According to an article by Kevin Kelleher published on Wired website, MySpace's membership skyrocketed from 20 million in 2005

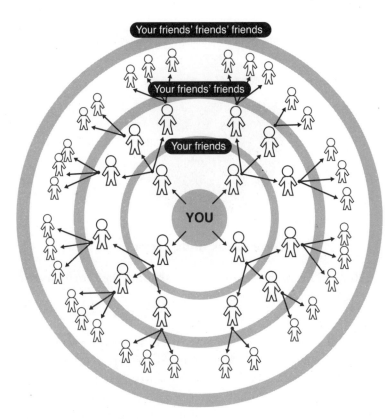

Figure 10.1   The social networking concept

to 225 million in 2008, an average annual growth rate of 513 per cent. Facebook grew by 550 per cent during the same period, while LinkedIn's rate was 182 per cent. According to Dave Roos, web information company Alexa reckons that seven of the top 20 most-visited websites in the world are social-networking sites such as MySpace or YouTube.

Social networking is an activity that 37 per cent of US adult internet users and 70 per cent of online teens engage in every month, and the numbers continue to grow. eMarketer projects that by 2011 half of online adults and 84 per cent of online teens in the United States will use social networking ('Social network marketing: ad spending and usage', published on eMarketer website).

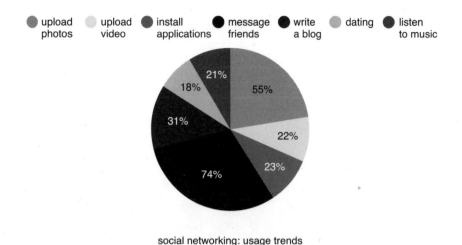

social networking: usage trends

Figure 10.2 The majority of people around the world use social networking to message friends

The myth that social networking sites are only for the young must be dispelled. Again according to Roos, ComScore reports that by August 2006 more than two-thirds of MySpace visitors were 25 years or older, with more than 40 per cent between the ages of 35 and 54.

Reflecting the internet itself, social networking sites are very global (Figure 10.3). Roos says that ComScore reports that in June 2007, 49 per cent of the visitors to Google's Orkut were from Latin America (many of them from Brazil) and 43 per cent came from the Asia-Pacific region. In the same month, 89 per cent of the visitors to Friendster were from the Asia-Pacific region, while 63 per cent of the visitors to Bebo were from Europe.

Facebook and MySpace rank among the most popular sites. But that's just the beginning. Social networking sites come in all sizes, shapes and colours. Niche networking sites are growing like wildfire.

Cafemom (a social network designed for mothers), LinkedIn (a site for professionals) and Fubar (the 'first online bar') grew tremendously between February 2007 and February 2008. Fubar exploded onto the scene from relative obscurity in a mere 12 months, testament to how quickly the social networking landscape can change.

Fashion social networks share opinions, information and gossip about what is happening in the fashion world. Share Your Look and

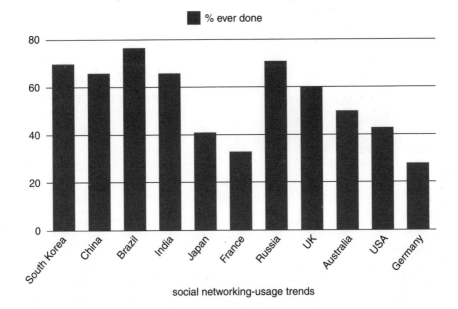

■ % ever done

social networking-usage trends

Figure 10.3   Social networking has caught on like wildfire every-where

StyleHive are stand-alone sites. MySpaceFashion is a niche of the blockbuster MySpace site.

You can find music social networks such as Pandora, LastFm and iLike.

LinkedIn attracts working professionals.

Black Planet, Asian Avenue and MiGente target various racial and ethnic affiliations.

Second Life is a virtual world; a twist on the social networking concept.

Other sites such as Yahoo! 360ÿ° and hi5 are general sites where users can form smaller groups based on interests or demographics.

Finally, there are famous sites like Flickr (Figure 10.4) and YouTube (Figure 10.5) which allow people to upload photos and videos.

Looking at a few big sites

Let's review some of the most well-known sites: Facebook, MySpace and LinkedIn.

Figure 10.4   The Flickr website allows you to upload and share your photos

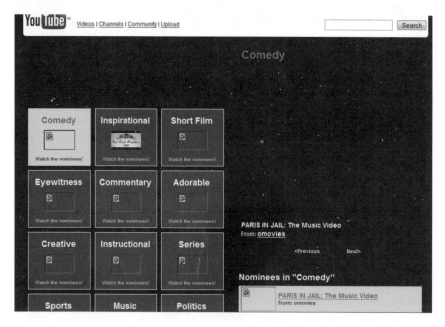

Figure 10.5   The famous YouTube site lets you share videos

Facebook

In 2004, three Harvard University students launched a website. Called thefacebook.com, the website's mission was to put students in touch, share photos and meet new people. The site quickly caught on at Harvard. Within 12 months, 800 college networks in the United States had joined. Membership grew to more than 5 million. In August 2005, the site's name was changed to Facebook.

Today anyone can join the network. While the scope of the site has expanded beyond students, its purpose remains the same – let people share information in an easy and entertaining way.

Facebook enjoys around 66 million users worldwide and the number grows exponentially (article by Aaron Ricadela published on BusinessWeek website). Facebook is not just for the young either. Only 30 per cent of all Facebook users are under the age of 24.

Many major corporations advertise on Facebook, including Blockbuster, CBS, Chase, Coca-Cola, Saturn, Sony Pictures, the New York Times and Verizon.

The Facebook site is attractive to big companies because it can match ads to an exact target market. Facebook gathers a lot of information from users when they sign on. This means that ads can be shown to a specific user based on sex, age, education, relationship status, keywords in their profile or even political views.

Linked In

LinkedIn positions itself as a social networking site for professionals and ranks as the largest social network of its kind. LinkedIn allows entrepreneurs and professionals to post profiles, make contacts and hunt for new jobs. With over 15 million members, LinkedIn is a growing phenomenon on the social networking scene.

LinkedIn profile pages read like résumés, summarizing professional experience and education as well as listing favourite books and bands. Until recently, users were unable to post a personal photograph. The reason for stopping this? LinkedIn did not want to lose its stature as a business site and become another excuse for online dating.

MySpace

MySpace is the biggest of all the social networking sites. Within four years of its 2003 launch, it enjoyed twice the traffic of Google (article by Julia Layton and Patrick Brothers published on HowStuffWorks website).

Why so successful? Many of the first people to use MySpace were musicians and bands. Undoubtedly, the music connection helped fuel growth.

Also, MySpace encourages freedom of expression without censorship. Almost anything goes except hate speech and extreme nudity.

Another factor which fuelled the growth of MySpace is the fact that it is extremely accessible and easily customized. Users can add music, video, graphics and new fonts. The MySpace 'Do what you want, we don't care' attitude attracts 16–25 year olds who make up a big proportion of MySpace users.

But MySpace is not just for young people. Thirty-, 40-, 50- and 70-somethings are all active. They use the site for all sorts of reasons: looking for new business, new dates, even to publish poetry. Bands use MySpace to get their music known. Established artists like Madonna use it to communicate with their fans.

In 2005, Rupert Murdoch's News Corp bought Intermix Media, the company that owned the controlling interest in MySpace, for $580 million.

Social networking benefits

Here are some of the benefits of social networking for a company:

- It moves you beyond your physical universe of bricks and mortar, opening up your world to new people and ideas.

- It helps you tear down organizational walls created by geographical or functional limitations.

- It helps you align the personal objectives of key individuals with the objectives of the organization.

- It enormously increases your brand equity.

- It boosts your marketing potential.

- It generates revenues.

- It allows you to source good talent – whether suppliers or employees.

- It facilitates cooperation between employees.

- It increases links to your original site, enhancing search engine optimization.

- It boosts traffic to your site.

- It changes your customer relationships. You will stop 'talking to' them and begin interacting with them.

The negatives of social networking

What are the negatives of social networking?

Social networking makes many business people feel vulnerable. CEOs worry about negative comments snowballing and creating a real public relations crisis for the company.

The reality is that if people want to speak negatively about you, they will. It doesn't matter if you are listening or not. If logic rules, it is better to know what they are saying about you than to remain in the dark.

Social networking requires a shift in thinking. It is essential to understand that these sites have nothing to do with the people or companies who build them. They are all about the people who use them.

A good example is a site called BlueShirtNation, an internal employee social networking site created by Best Buy Corporation. Launched by Gary Koelling and Steve Bendt, the site originally set out to gain more in-depth information about the Best Buy consumer from the sales associates.

But according to Albert Maruggi, Koelling and Bendt were taken aback by the employee response. 'It wasn't what we thought it was going to be about. It was about what the users thought it was going to be about. They basically told us what they wanted, saying if you want us to participate, build it like this,' says Bendt.

And the results?

Around 18,000 Best Buy employees participate in the community. The employees using the site range from senior managers to on-the-floor sales associates.

Relations between floor employees and managers are closer than ever. The site achieved its initial objective and provides excellent, in-depth insights into the consumer.

The site's biggest benefit is improved relations between employees and the company. Better communications have helped to change policies ranging from customer service to the employee discount programme.

According to Koelling, BlueShirtNation has made the company less hierarchical, shifting ownership of the company towards its users. Because of this, buy-in to company objectives is much better.

'Corporations are in business to make money', Koelling says. 'However, there are a lot of voices out there that could contribute to that end goal, that might not get a chance to participate in the typical hierarchical structure.'

The widget phenomenon

Widgets – small bundles of software – can be downloaded and customized. Used by millions of social networkers, widgets help users customize their profiles or communicate with their friends.

According to a new method of calculation by ComScore (Ricadela, 2008), 586 million individual internet users viewed a piece of widget software in November 2007.

A growing list of companies use widgets to spread their message or raise brand loyalty: Blockbuster, Electronic Arts, Gap, Hallmark, Hewlett-Packard, Paramount Pictures, Sony Pictures and Viacom.

Many believe widgets do a better job than banner ads. 'Content and functionality are the new creativity – it's not about whether you have a whiz-bang rich media banner running', states Andy Batement, CEO of brand consultancy Interbrand New York (Ricadela; see above).

As recent Silicon Valley start-ups, Slide and RockYou are two of the biggest players in the widget game. The two companies create fun software which lets users on social networking sites make slide shows, compare friends or scrawl messages on each other's home pages. Slide and RockYou are currently waging a major PR war for both users and advertisers. 'It's like Coke and Pepsi', according to Jeremy Liew, a general partner at Lightspeed Venture Partners, a RockYou investor (Aaron Ricadela; see above).

Widget development is rife with risks. Jeremiah Owyang, a well-known Forrester analyst, recommends that businesses begin by first sponsoring existing successful widgets. After this they can consider building their own. But because widgets are altogether different from creating a traditional website, brands should lean on experts to build and manage them.

Widgets represent an attractive new market for advertisers, although some big companies are reticent.

Dell Computers and widgets

In January 2008, Dell Computers created a successful one-week long 'green' campaign using an existing widget (Graffiti) on Facebook. All Graffiti members were asked to create art based on the theme of 'What does green mean to you?' The prize was an environmentally friendly 22-inch Dell monitor.

In this case, Dell leveraged a pre-existing, popular application situated in a robust community. Graffiti enjoys a high popular rating (four stars out of five) and 177,000 users.

The highly successful event lasted one short week. Over 7,000 pieces of artwork were created and submitted. The works were wide-ranging, with artists expressing the variety of what the concept of green meant to them.

Voting for the winner started during the second week, with one million votes cast. In this truly global competition, the winners came from all over the world: Canada, the Maldives, Sweden and the United States.

The contest distinguished Dell from other companies that continue to do traditional online ads. The widget-based campaign caught on quickly as the community totally took charge. The community participated, created the art and determined the winners. The best news for Dell? The campaign not only drove users to Dell's microsite on Facebook, it also boosted traffic to Dell's corporate website.

For Dell, widgets is a winning word.

A&E Television Networks and widgets

A&E Television Networks also experimented with widgets, using a widget to promote a new series called *Parking Wars*.

A&E built an online game (ie a widget) based on *Parking Wars*. Introduced in mid-December 2007, the game, played on Facebook, allowed users to park virtual cars on a friend's profile pages or 'streets'. Players could then give tickets to those cars parked on their page.

The game attracted 200,000 unique users by the first quarter of 2008, with many repeat players. In total, it generated an impressive 45 million page views (article by Rachael King published on BusinessWeek website).

Sony and widgets

Sony promoted the film *Resident Evil* by using a RockYou zombies application. The application sends virtual zombies to bite the sender's friends. Originally estimating that 10,000 people would sign up, Sony was shocked – but pleased – to see that the final number was closer to 1 million people (King; see above).

TripAdvisor and widgets

TripAdvisor chose to build their own application. Installed by 7.8 million people at its peak, TripAdvisor's Cities I've Visited is a map where people show where they have travelled. It only took two people about three days to build this successful application (King; see above).

The future of widgets

Widgets are not yet a huge advertising or branding force. The widget market remains very young and small. According to eMarketer, US web widget and application ad spending will total $40 million in 2008, 2.5 per cent of the $1.6 billion estimated for online social network ad spending (King; see above).

The future of widgets is unclear. On the one hand, once there are industry standard metrics and you can measure the success or failure of a widget, widgets could very well transform the face of social networking. On the other hand, widgets may fade into the background, just another internet fad.

To successfully and continuously engage the user remains the big challenge for widgets. 'It's very challenging to maintain someone's interest over a long period of time,' says Debra Aho Williamson, a senior analyst at eMarketer. 'Applications and widgets have a pretty short shelf life' (King; see above). The widgets with longer lifespans are those where developers continually add new features to seduce users to return.

Build your own network or go with a pre-existing one?

Many companies find hosting a community very attractive. A community is synonymous with a marketplace. Created correctly, the network should do the marketing for you. Examples would be social networking sites launched by Channel9 for Microsoft, Big Brothers and Sisters, Dell, Microsoft, Intel, Carnival Cruise Lines and Wal-Mart.

What is the purpose of building your own network when so many networks already exist?

Control. Many companies believe they can control things better if the community is their own.

Another reason companies decide to create their own social networking sites is because the functionality on sites like Facebook and MySpace is limited. For example, a company that creates its own site may want a more private environment; many users don't want to participate in a public space.

Your own social networking site will help build trust. You can develop a relationship with your consumers and float ideas by them. This is less possible in a traditional open network.

The negative side of having your own community is the glut of social networking sites. As more and more social networking sites appear, it will become more and more difficult to ask users to fill out yet another profile.

When you create your own site, it may be tempting to shape the social networking experience. Make sure you listen first rather than pushing content out.

When deciding between creating your own community or going with a pre-existing one, ask your consumer. Do they already participate in a community online? Are they happy with that community? Don't forget to fish where the fish are.

An example of a company that has done their own social networking site is LEGO Mindstorm. Another is Charles Schwab.

The answer is that most companies will do both. They will participate on sites like MySpace and Facebook. But they will also build social networking tools into corporate sites. The objective of these social networking sites is to build loyalty while at the same time creating an online place where people want to hang out. Nike has a community called Joga which gathers soccer fans together from all over the world. And they will participate in pre-existing communities.

How to build your own network

How do you build your own social network? The online service Ning.com allows an individual or company to build a social network around a specific theme. Using Ning, a company can build a social network around their brand or market. An individual can use it to build a more tightly focused community on a larger social networking site.

There are risks to custom-building a social network. According to Rusty Weston, Rodney Rumford, CEO of Gravitational Media, points out: 'The question to ask yourself is – is it worth the time, effort and money to create [a custom social network] yourself or can you leverage what already exists in Facebook for a much lower cost and quicker time to market? If there's unique functionality that Facebook doesn't offer, then building your own might be the option.'

You can build a custom social network for customers or prospects, employees or suppliers. Many people believe that the ROI on employee social networks may be superior. Internal social networks can help you get the most out of high-value employees. It will help make them happier and retain their loyalty.

Take a cue from the US presidential campaign

The 2008 US presidential campaign illustrates creative uses of social media marketing. All the candidates used YouTube, MySpace and Facebook. Some used Twitter, a microblogging service allowing users to send and receive short text messages via multiple sources including computers and mobile phones.

John Edwards was a trailblazer when he announced his candidacy on YouTube. But Barack Obama led the pack with his creation of a social network called MyBarackObama.com. This first-of-its-kind politically oriented social network allowed users to create profiles, bringing together current and prospective Obama supporters in an environment controlled by the candidate himself.

There is nothing stopping companies of all sizes from doing the exact same thing, ie developing their own brand-hosted community.

Disappointing advertising performance of social networks

According to eMarketer, worldwide online social network ad spending is expected to grow by 81 per cent from $1.2 billion in 2007 to $2.2 billion in 2008. Social network ad spending should soar to $4.1 billion in 2011 ('Social network marketing: ad spending and usage'; see above).

Still, the 2008 number represents only 6 per cent of all online ad spending. And only a tiny amount of the money will be devoted to widget software. According to Will Price, Managing Director of Hummer Winblad Venture Partners, advertisers will spend $20–40 million on advertisements linked to widget software in 2008 (Ricadela; see above).

Despite the stunning popularity of social networking, advertising has not performed nearly as well as anticipated. Having said that, the growth of ad spend on social networking sites is not unimpressive. For example, in 2008, the growth of the larger and more mature total online advertising sector grew by 22 per cent while social networking grew by 72 per cent (article by Mark Sweney published on guardian.co.uk).

According to Debra Aho Williamson, eMarketer's senior analyst specializing in social networking, 'Social networking websites are still trying to figure out what sort of advertising works. Tapping into consumers' conversations and spreading brand awareness virally has proven more challenging than companies originally thought' (Sweney; see above).

Even Google is stumped, unable to figure out how best to capitalize on the enormous audiences these social networking sites represent. Google's Sergey Brin says: 'I don't think we have the killer best way to advertise and monetize the social networks yet' (Kevin Kelleher; see above).

Social networking captures 21st-century trends

The meteoric growth of the various social networking sites should tell us something.

People like to belong to communities. People want to connect.

As institutions and relationships disintegrate in our everyday lives, we seek comfort in connecting with people in any way we can. During a worldwide global study I conducted for ASSA ABLOY, this theme was repeated in Australia, China, the United States, Africa and all over Europe. When all else is torn away, the only thing we have left is the comfort of family and friends – even virtual ones. It is the fact that social networking sites build on this trend that makes them so strong. It is why they must not be ignored.

The next generation will be smaller and more focused

The next generation of consumer social networks will be much smaller and far more focused, and will help all types and sizes of marketers. Already there are social network sites devoted to topics as diverse as wine clubs, sports clubs and recipe exchanges.

Social networking should be a feature of sites, not their sole destination. The one-size-fits-all model of Facebook and MySpace will give way to lots of narrowly focused websites with social networking built in.

To date, online communities have existed as stand-alone destinations. In the future, they will be the web's equivalent of running water or electricity.

Everyone is searching for the successor to MySpace or Facebook. It looks like the next big community is not one single destination. It is going to be everywhere.

Social networking is going to be 'like air'.

The transition of community from a few big-reach sites to a ubiquitous platform is not necessarily good news for marketers. It makes social network advertising – which is already not that great – even more difficult.

You can either join in on other communities or create your own destinations. If you join in on another organization's community, the advantage is that it already has members that come to it regularly. But you may not be able to find the exact community you need, so you may be forced to create your own.

Many marketers experiment with social media via the large online communities. However, it is often difficult to reach relevant audiences through such mass-media environments. Very often, the smaller social networking sites work better.

For example, many users will visit their professional community like iToolbox and LinkedIn several times a day. To many, such a community is a utility, a desktop tool that is part of their daily workflow.

Communities challenge traditional thinking

Communities go against the grain of traditional companies' way of doing business and marketing. Instead of control, a company will host social interaction. It is the customer rather than the company that develops most of the content.

A solid, working community will share, involve influencers as well as customers who may become co-creators with your company. Co-creation is when people love your products or services so much they want to build on top of something you've already done. Co-creation is extremely powerful. But it can be equally intimidating for companies who are used to doing all the thinking for their customers.

Simply put, it requires a change in mindset.

Social networking sites are not a passing fad. If you ignore them, you will miss out on transforming your business, increasing revenue, finding and developing talent as well as making your business run more efficiently.

Social networking is not going away. Embrace it. Social networking will be like air. And you will want to be sure to be breathing it.

Summary

- Social networking will be like air.
- Social networking is not just for the young.
- You can create your own social network or piggyback onto a big site like MySpace.
- Advertising on social networks is still problematic. Engage the community instead.
- Social networking is powerful; it reflects a key trend of the 21st century, which is that people want to connect.

11 Viral velocity

Understanding how to create a viral marketing campaign that works

Figure 11.1   The idea behind viral marketing is very simple

Tiny waves on a big pond...

A carefully designed viral marketing strategy resembles tiny waves spreading ever farther, like a single pebble dropped into a pond (article by Ralph F Wilson published on Web Marketing Today website).

According to social scientists, each person has a network of 8–12 people in their close network of friends, family and colleagues. A broader social network can range into the hundreds or even thousands. If you place your message into an existing communications network, things will multiply rapidly (Wilson; see above).

The magic of viral

Viral marketing is a powerful but little-understood online marketing tool.

The magic of viral marketing is that, with little effort, your message spreads exponentially, while traffic to your website soars. Like a biological virus, a viral marketing campaign is contagious. Everyone will want to see it. Everyone will want to share it.

The ultimate marketing tool

Viral marketing is an ideal way to promote your online business. If successful, hundreds of people will carry your promotion out for you.

The ultimate in marketing, viral marketing lets you get your message out quickly with a small budget and maximum effect. With a pinch of money and a dash of creativity, you will dramatically impact both the thinking and behaviour of your target market.

Viral marketing is not new

Viral marketing is not new. It has been around forever. According to experts, a satisfied customer tells an average of three people about a product or service he likes. Conversely, he will tell eleven people about a product or service he does not like (Wikipedia). Viral marketing takes advantage of this natural phenomenon.

If you're an art lover, I'm sure you would say Picasso was doing viral marketing in the Paris salons by having one piece shown which would make an impact, thereby leading people to want more. In essence you are doing the same thing: viral content – or in [Picasso's] case a painting – is being put out there where your peers are, where everyone is collecting, and you know people are going to be paying attention to what's produced.

The principle is old but the medium is what makes it possible for companies of all sizes to engage in it.

Rand Fishkin, reported by Rachelle Money in article published on Wordtracker.com

Hot viral marketing is getting hotter

The internet, with its speed and immediacy, heats up viral marketing. According to one venture capital firm, 80 per cent of new business plans have the words 'viral marketing' in them.

Once again, mass marketing is turned on its head by viral marketing.

Instead of spending a lot, you spend nothing.

Instead of pushing out a message, you let your fans do your work for you.

Executed well, viral marketing delivers 1,000 times more impact than regular advertising. Viral marketing has grown out of the increased cynicism towards mass marketing, which has coincided with new social tools on the internet.

Viral marketing believes it is consumers – not companies – that influence brand creation. The idea is that no one pays attention to the mass-marketer message. They prefer to discover brands on their own. The company takes a back seat to consumers in communicating what a brand stands for.

The greatest internet success stories don't advertise their products. They depend instead on viral marketing. If you see a site or product relying on advertising to get the word out, they have probably not yet fully embraced Web 2.0.

What are viral marketing's benefits?

Viral marketing gives you many benefits:

- It costs next to nothing.

- It runs itself.
- Its effect is immediate.
- You can receive a lot of publicity for your site in a short period of time.
- It is fresh and new (versus a more worn mass-marketing approach).
- It provides good link bait.

A word about link bait

What is a link bait?

- Link bait attracts people to your site. It refers to content which is created with the goal of getting people to link to it.
- Link bait increases search and referral traffic to a site. If this traffic is monetized, it can ultimately add to sales or ad revenue.
- Link bait is about good content.
- A good link bait tool will create 'brand evangelists' – people who will talk positively about you.
- Link bait works best when it adds value to the website.
- Link bait comes in many forms: an entertaining article, a useful application or a list of helpful resources.
- Link bait works well if it relates to popular topics or cultural events relevant at a specific time.
- Link bait shouldn't look like link bait. Otherwise, it looks like you are trying too hard for links. The link bait should feel natural.
- Good link bait is also driven by passion.

A good example of link bait is Burger King's Subservient Chicken campaign. This campaign created a lot of awareness, made the brand 'cool' and introduced a whole new generation to Burger King.

The creation of a viral campaign

How do you create a viral marketing campaign?

Your viral marketing campaign requires a great product. You can get ideas by looking carefully at your industry and listening to what people are saying.

You need to provide something that is free. It can be a free product or service such as e-mail service, information or software.

Viral content can be a blog post, a diagram, a video, a photograph, an article, an e-book, a widget or graphics.

Viral marketing is not exclusive. Get it out there for everyone to see. Tap into the community with the biggest potential to spread your content. Post it on a forum, write a blog or vote for it on Reddit, Delicious or Digg, e-mail it to friends or text it through Twitter. Use other social media platforms like MySpace and Facebook where your brand will get maximum exposure.

Keep spin to a minimum. Don't create your viral marketing campaign with your public relations department. People will reject anything that feels artificial, controlled or created to comply with communication guidelines. Every time you give your PR department content to edit, your content will very likely not succeed. Your PR department will rip the soul out of it, diluting its authenticity (Money; see above).

Be natural, irreverent and quirky instead.

Make it easy, not hard! Easy to read, easy to get, easy to understand. If people need to fill out millions of forms or click too many times, you will lose them. Do not require people to register, become members, download special software, unlock codes or do something in order to get to the right link.

The whole point of a viral campaign is sharing. People need to be able to share the content easily with their friends and family. You can help the process along with an incentive. Viral marketing always works better when there is a tangible incentive.

A viral marketing campaign should always tap into important, common human motivations.

A viral marketing campaign should be based on a good idea. Figure out what your users are passionate about.

Make absolutely sure your idea has not been used before.

Think about how your viral marketing campaign might benefit your users.

Send users to an excellent site. The whole point of viral marketing is to increase traffic and maximize conversion. This is impossible if you send users to a mediocre site.

Do research. Find out who in your industry has had successes in viral marketing and who has failed.

Brainstorm. Pick your best ideas. Execute them. Show them to a sample audience.

Push it out. E-mail bloggers, submit to social media sites, post a twitter, e-mail to friends.

Leave it out there even if nothing happens. It could be 'found' later.

Kill content if you are getting a lot of negative feedback.

Make sure video content is easy to share and spread. Make it easy to link to your URL. Make sure people link to your site rather than YouTube for videos.

Finally, it should be easily scalable so it can transit from a small user base to a large one with ease.

If your first campaign is successful, create a sequel.

Link, link, link.

Viral products you can create

What kinds of viral products can you create?

Create a viral e-book. Let your website visitors give your free e-book away to others.

Set up a forum or discussion board. Let people use this for their own website. Brand yourself at the top.

Create a template or graphics and upload them to your site. People can then give these away. Ensure your name is on them or at least require people to link directly to your website.

Write articles relating to your product or service. Let people reprint your articles on their website, in their e-zine, e-newsletter or e-book. Include your resource box and an option for article reprints at the bottom of each article.

Buy products that will sell you a licence so you can distribute a product free of charge to other people. Be sure the products provide branding rights. You can include your own name, website and contact information.

Create a video. The video can be funny. Or informative. Or both. Ensure each video contains your URL before you post it to a site like YouTube. People *love* funny videos.

Run a competition. Offer cash prizes or free advertising to the person who sends you the most traffic. This method offers you traffic and back links as well (based on '6 ideas for viral marketing', article published on the Everything About Marketing website).

Content can take many forms. But it must be easy to spread and must attract the right type of audience. This audience has been nick-named the 'linkorati', ie the community with the maximum potential to spread your content (Money; see above). The linkorati take content they enjoy and spread it throughout the internet by posting it on forums or blogs, linking to it, voting for it on Reddit, Delicious or Digg, text messaging it through Twitter or e-mailing it to their friends.

Why some viral campaigns work

You can throw a burning match into a forest. The forest might ignite. Or it might not. It will depend on the condition of the forest. This is an important lesson when you launch a viral marketing campaign.

Viral marketing is unpredictable. It is hard to know which campaigns will work and which won't. Some fail miserably. Some succeed beyond people's wildest expectations. Your viral marketing campaign must be entertaining, relevant, new and fresh and exclusive.

One thing is for sure. You need to do it right. Or don't do it at all. Only the best viral marketing campaigns make it.

There is no sure-fire way to success. Expect to strike out a few times before being successful (Money; see above).

Viral marketing is about emotion

Viral marketing is 100 per cent about emotion. Make people feel something. Make them angry. Love or hate. Laugh or cry.

Make their adrenalin run.

Be controversial. Don't try to please everyone. Have an edge.

Surprise. Do something unexpected.

Everyone tries to be cool. Don't try to be cool. It is banal.

Never, ever, copy someone else. You will fall flat on your face.

Examples of successful viral marketing campaigns

Hotmail

The classic example of a viral marketing campaign is Hotmail. Using viral marketing, Hotmail grew a subscriber base faster than any other company in history. They employed a straightforward strategy. Hotmail gave away a free web-based e-mail account with a tag line at the bottom of every outgoing e-mail that read, 'Get your free, private e-mail at www.hotmail.com.'

Within three years, Hotmail had 40 million users. A hundred and fifty thousand people signed up every day.

Blendtec

Another campaign is the famous Blendtec one with its 'Will it blend?' videos. In these short videos, Blendtec blended everything from golf balls and credit cards to an iPhone in their industrial-strength blenders. A great success, the campaign brought enormous attention to a product most people did not even know existed.

The film Cloverfield

This campaign started with the release of a teaser trailer. It omitted the title of the movie, giving only the release date. The online viral marketing campaign was very complex, blending a series of fictitious company websites to MySpace profiles for the film's main characters.

Dove Evolution

This breakthrough campaign was wildly popular. It comprised short films showing how fashion beauty is artificially manufactured. The idea was to tell women that they shouldn't condemn themselves if they don't measure up to a standard of beauty that is in itself falsely attained (Figure 11.2).

Cadbury Dairy Milk 2007 gorilla advertisement

The Cadbury gorilla video captivated millions with its music and dramatic drum-playing gorilla (Figure 11.3).

Figure 11.2   The Dove Evolution viral marketing campaign

Figure 11.3   The Cadbury Dairy Milk viral marketing campaign

Sporting Portugal

In 2007, the Portuguese football club Sporting Portugal launched a viral marketing campaign for season seats. A video required the user to input their name and phone number before they could view the playback. The video featured the coach Paulo Bento and the players in the locker room. The coach makes a phone call to the user saying they can't start the season until the user buys a season ticket. The campaign was a totally new experience with perfectly synchronized phone and video. It led to 200,000 page views in less than 24 hours.

BMW

One way of creating a compelling campaign is to tell a good story. BMW is an excellent example. The film it used, which recounts the gripping story of a war journalist, holds the viewer spellbound from start to finish. And importantly, the campaign is utterly non-promotional; the name BMW never once appears on the screen.

Sony Bravia

The captivating and moving video campaign for Sony Bravia televisions went one step further than BMW and did not even show the product.

The Gobbledegook Manifesto

Here is another example of a viral campaign. It was created by David Meerman Scott, who wrote an article about the wishy-washy language that corporations love to use. He listed examples like 'flexible', 'robust', 'turnkey' and 'best of breed'. Scott put all the gobbledegook language in a book, sent it to a friend and issued a press release listing some of the most offensive words. The ROI for this campaign was reportedly $50,000 in new business. The campaign itself cost only a few hundred dollars.

World of Warcraft

Video advertisements feature actors like Jean-Claude Van Damme, Verne Troyer and William Shatner who talk about the characters they play in the game. The campaign enjoyed hundreds of thousands of views on YouTube.

Apple

Two men acting as a PC and a Mac talk with each other. A perfect example where content created for advertising becomes a viral campaign.

Those viral campaigns that went wrong

Starbucks

In August 2006, Starbucks sent an e-mail coupon for free iced coffee to their employees in the southeast United States (Figure 11.4). The company asked them to forward the e-mail coupon to their friends and family. Not intending this to be a viral marketing campaign, Starbucks was utterly stumped when, within hours, the coupon had

Figure 11.4 The ill-fated Starbucks viral marketing campaign

spread across the internet like wildfire. The campaign ended up reaching a much larger audience than Starbucks originally intended.

The problem started when Starbucks decided not to honour the coupons. So, instead of building goodwill with their client base and even potentially introducing new consumers to their product, they issued the following:

> *An e-mail offering a free Starbucks iced coffee was distributed to a limited group of Starbucks partners (employees) in the southeast United States on Wednesday, August 23, 2006 with instructions to forward to their group of friends and family. Unfortunately, it has been redistributed beyond the original intent and modified beyond Starbucks control. Effective immediately, this offer will no longer be valid at any Starbucks locations.*
>
> *We apologize for any confusion and inconvenience as a result of this offer.*

Seeing their blunder, Caribou Coffee, a Starbucks competitor, announced that *they* would honour the coupons themselves. Clearly a much better response!

Chevy Apprentice – create an ad

It sounded like a good idea. Chevy and *The Apprentice* TV show decided to team up to promote the new Chevy Tahoe. They set it up so that website visitors could create their own Chevy Tahoe advertisement. The users were allowed to take stock footage and insert their own captions.

The idea wasn't bad. The problem started when the ads went live with no one reviewing them (Figure 11.5).

Even better, Chevy left the videos up on the site for everyone to see.

The negative side of viral marketing

What is the bad thing about viral marketing?

Many people believe that the viral model is flawed. Listed below are some of the issues surrounding viral marketing:

- *The quality of communication.* The question is: is simply *any* communication good as long as it is retold? Is just getting people to talk

Figure 11.5 The Chevy Tahoe viral marketing campaign didn't exactly help the brand

about something a goal? Isn't it better to have an important message? One that your company or brand should stand for? Or a message that affects how people think about themselves or the world? Are we looking to create any old communication or communication with a meaning?

Many people believe that viral marketing is fashion marketing. Here today, gone tomorrow. A fad. It seeks to influence the taste-makers. To become *the* thing to watch. Until a newer, better idea shows up.

- *No control.* You exercise no control over who will see your message. You might get a lot of views. A lot of people may share your content. But is your message really being seen by your target audience?

- *Altered message.* In the process of going viral, there is always the risk that your message could be changed. This could ultimately negatively impact your brand perception.

- *Difficulty in tracking and measurement.* Viral marketing campaigns are notoriously difficult to track and measure.

- *Spam.* Viral marketing can potentially lead to a large-scale spam problem, which could damage your reputation.

- *Length of time the campaign stays out there.* Can you control how long your message remains out there? How long can it stay out before it gets boring or distorted?

Reacting to consumer-generated viral content

Viral content is inextricably linked with online reputation management. It isn't always *you* creating the videos. People can create content about you without you knowing. It is essential to be able to react quickly to consumer-generated viral content – whether good or bad. You must not get caught unprepared.

Here are two examples.

Diet Coke and Mentos

One of the most well-known viral campaigns, the Diet Coke and Mentos video was launched by two friends on a Saturday (Figure 11.6). The video showed what happened when you mix Mentos with Diet Coke. By Monday morning, the two had been contacted by David Letterman.

And Mentos.

Mentos reacted quickly.

Coke didn't.

Mentos began shipping thousands of mints for their experiments.

Coke's initial reaction was tepid, with Coke spokeswoman Susan McDermott saying, 'We would hope people want to drink [Diet Coke] more than try to experiment with it.'

Coke clearly didn't get it.

The original video received more than two million views. The video did even better at Revver, where it was originally posted. Mentos spends about $20 million per year on US advertising. They estimate the worth of the videos at $10 million. That nets out to a full 50 per cent gain in advertising value... without paying a cent!

JetBlue

When an ice storm hit the US east coast, JetBlue airline travellers were stranded in airports and on runways as more than 1,000 JetBlue flights were grounded.

Figure 11.6 The Diet Coke and Mentos video showed what can happen to you when you least expect it

Trapped passengers spent over six hours on the tarmac in grounded planes. Others were stranded in terminals for days. JetBlue's 11,000 pilots and flight attendants struggled to communicate with the ground staff. Call centres crushed with phone calls were manned by staff poorly trained to handle such a widespread crisis.

Videos of the JetBlue nightmare cropped up all over YouTube.

The crisis began to subside when JetBlue CEO David Neeleman apologized on YouTube. He outlined 7- and 30-day plans to put new policies in place. In interviews with other news outlets, Neeleman acknowledged flaws in JetBlue's corporate structure. He explained the failure of the system and vowed to fix things.

The company offered immediate refunds and travel vouchers to customers stuck on planes for over three hours. And, for good measure, JetBlue distributed a Customer Bill of Rights, which is unique among US airlines (article by Jennifer Laycock published on SearchEngineGuide.com).

The conclusion? Viral opportunities or challenges can appear out of the blue – and are often out of your control. You must be prepared to deal with them at a moment's notice. Ignore them at your risk.

Summary

- Viral marketing is an excellent weapon for fast exposure.
- Viral marketing runs itself.
- Viral marketing costs nothing.
- Be prepared for consumer-generated viral activity about your brand, and be sure to react quickly and positively.
- Viral marketing is all about emotion – so pick your emotional message carefully.

12 Video opens the floodgates

Getting ready for the future of the video-based internet

The potential for everyone to self-publish has the ability to revolutionize the world.

Katie Dean in article published on the Wired.com website

The world is becoming video

As Reid Hoffman at LinkedIn has said, bringing video to online is similar to the print-to-television revolution:

Suddenly this is a much more emotionally and socially engaging medium. There is much more social interaction for me to be watching someone's own little music video than to be reading a long blog post.

Quoted by Weber, 2007

Video offers the best way for you to share your image and personality

You can find no better way to share your image and personality than with video. A powerful interactive tool, video creates strong memories because it touches several senses at the same time. Even better, online video delivers a branding image for a tiny fraction of the cost of a TV commercial any time 24 hours a day, seven days a week, worldwide.

All the different ways video can be used on the internet

Video on the internet can be used in many different ways. There are video podcasts, the visual extension of audio podcasting. Video podcasts are called videocasts, vidcasts and vodcasts. We have video blogs, which are called vlogs. And we also have video that can be used for viral marketing, using sites like YouTube to carry content to millions of viewers.

The video explosion

But no matter what form it takes and whatever we call it, the use of video on the internet is exploding. Broadband penetration and YouTube are the two main drivers of this explosion. During a networking breakfast called 'Economics of the New Television Marketplace', the Jack Myers consultancy predicted that by 2012, 40 per cent of all video consumption will occur outside the television set (Michael Learmonth in article published on Silicon Alley Insider website).

A Universal McCann study carried out in three waves showed an explosive rise in the percentage of people who watched video clips from September 2006 to March 2008 (see Table 12.1).

User-generated videos (UGVs) tallied 22 billion views worldwide in 2007, up 70 per cent over 2006, according to Accustream iMedia Research's UGV 2005–2008 'Mania Meets Mainstream' report.

And surprisingly, despite a slight bias towards the 18–29-year-old internet user, the general online video audience is broad and stretches

Table 12.1 The use of video is exploding around the world

	Sep 06 (%)	June 07 (%)	Mar 08 (%)
Global	32	63	83
Australia	25	58	77
China	56	79	89
France	23	54	63
Germany	20	44	77
Italy	35	63	78
Russia	22	58	68
South Korea	30	74	86
Spain	28	69	87
UK	33	61	85
USA	32	52	74

Source: Universal McCann

across all age groups, according to the Annual Gadgets Survey 2007 by the Pew Internet & American Life Project.

The Online Publishers Association reports that 7 out of 10 internet users have watched an online video and 30 per cent of those people have shared one with friends, usually via e-mail.

The conclusion? Online video viewing is widespread among internet users of all ages. Equally, the watching of video clips is a global phenomenon (Figure 12.1).

But while the number of people who watch videos staggers the mind, the number of people who are actually creating and uploading videos is much smaller (Figure 12.2).

Finally, video is exploding in terms of advertising. eMarketer expects online video advertising to reach $1 billion in 2008 and nearly $3 billion by 2010.

Video brings new dimensions to marketers and consumers alike

Video entices marketers because, unlike television ads, video allows you to talk to highly targeted audiences. Video allows you to explore niche subjects traditionally ignored by 'big media'.

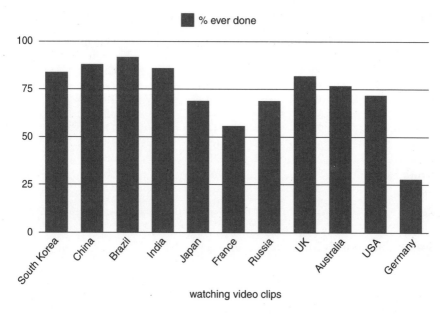

Figure 12.1 Video is very popular around the globe

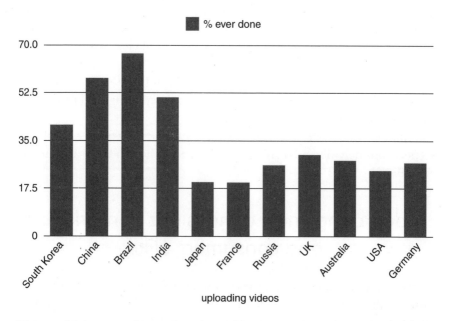

Figure 12.2 People tend to be video spectators rather than video creators

> When you have Hollywood and major media as a filter, they're going to do what appeals to millions rather than thousands. It's just not cost-effective for them to produce a show about the didgeridoo (for example). That's what the internet has changed – you can find stuff and market it ridiculously cheaply.
>
> Katie Dean; see above

'You can really serve a niche much better than traditional television', says David Prager, Chief Operating Officer and VP of programming at Revision3, an online television network that shows video podcasts.

If audio opened the doors for the democratization of media, video is opening the floodgates.

We are no longer compelled to watch what traditional broadcasters tell us to watch. In addition, we see once again how consumers have moved beyond consumption: consumers are simultaneously consumers and producers.

Steve Garfield, nicknamed the father of video blogging, comments on these changes:

> People who are normally just passive consumers of video are gonna say 'Whoa, we can create it and we can get it out there the same way the big networks are getting it out... There are no barriers to entry, of cost or distribution. It's available to anybody. There are stories to be told. And there are lots of stories out there... As more and more people figure out how to put video on the web, you'll get a lot more stories bubbling up.'
>
> Quoted by Mike Miliard in article published on the Boston Phoenix website

Small businesses become big with video

Video on the internet evens out the playing field. In the past, only big businesses could access expensive studios that produced sophisticated advertisements. Today, even a company of one can create high-quality media. Cheap digital cameras, free editing software, video-hosting services and increased broadband penetration have all made production and publishing extremely easy. RSS aggregation makes it simple for viewers to find their favourite videos and videocasts.

Diversity is the spice of life

And as we move from being media consumers to being media makers, the variety of videos available will be mind-boggling. 'We're going from being media consumers to media makers. We're learning how to do that', says Chuck Olsen, a documentary film maker and video blogger from Minnesota. 'There's sort of a whole continuum between [videotaping] grandpa's birthday and film making' (Dean; see above).

The quality and content of video vary wildly. Some videos are thrown together and are rather rough. Others, meticulously put together, distinguish themselves with careful edits and excellent music selection. Like audio podcasts, subjects range from talk shows to footage about strangers' lives. Authors come from all walks of life. The tone of voice can vary from hilariously funny to dead serious.

There are endless uses of videos:

- Incorporate them in your blogs to showcase your products/services.

- Create viral videos. By attracting large audiences, you will drive heavy traffic to your site.

- Hold online video conferences.

- Make how-to videos which explain market trends or how your product works.

The Blendtec example

The story of Blendtec is a good example of video online. The marketing director of Blendtec, George Wright, faced a big challenge. The Blendtec blender price tag of $400 rendered consumers speechless – and unable to open their wallets. In the quest for a marketing answer, Wright visited the company's development lab. There he was dumbstruck as he watched Blendtec's amazing pulverization capabilities. On seeing these, he realized that nothing would sell the blender better than a visual demonstration of the blender's powers. He duly created an in-house video and posted it on YouTube. The video took off as a sensation (Figure 12.3).

The first video showed a chicken and a Coca-Cola being pulverized. Blendtec graduated to a whole series of demonstrations from marbles to tiki torches. The destruction of an iPod proved to be the most popular video of all.

All the attention translated into the bottom line: consumer sales have increased fivefold since the videos appeared.

The Blendtec campaign remains a classic internet video success story. The videos worked because they contained some crucial ingredients: they were funny, visually arresting, short, authentic, original and connected to the value of the product.

Video can also be used in blogs

The integration of video into blogs (vlogs) is increasingly popular. One of the best-known video blogs is Rocketboom which puts together an irreverent daily news programme.

Figure 12.3 The Blendtec video campaign was a wild success

Li Walker, an analyst with the Yankee Group, believes vlogs will supplement traditional broadcasting, just like written blogs have become an extension of traditional media (Dean; see above).

According to Steve Garfield, companies should use vlogs to assist their customers. It is an easy way to showcase your product and its special features. Only a moving image illustrates exactly how your product works. At long last, give three dimensions to your products through videos.

Enter YouTube

YouTube's exploding popularity has fuelled the video craze. YouTube's popularity means that your video can be potentially viewed by a lot of people. When people like your video, they embed it into their own sites or blogs and your video's exposure booms.

Having said this, YouTube is not perfect.

One of the biggest concerns about video sharing on a site like YouTube is that users are not obliged to come to your site to see the video. Even if your video enjoys wild popularity, it may not build traffic to your site. It is essential you give viewers an incentive to visit your site once they have viewed your video.

Another option is that you can change the video settings so they can't be viewed on the YouTube site or if embedded on another site. In other words, the video can only be viewed on your site. The problem with this is that it will greatly limit the viewers who see your video.

Another negative about uploading your video to YouTube and then embedding it in your site is that this will include the logo of YouTube on your video. Although unobtrusive, this can be perceived as unprofessional.

If you decide to avoid YouTube altogether, you can upload your video to your own server and embed it from there. This will definitely give you more control over your video but has some disadvantages. The first is that visitors will need a browser plug-in to view it. While plug-ins tend to be free to download, many users can't be bothered to download them. The second disadvantage is that video files are very large. If you make your video available from your server, you will take up valuable file storage space.

Aside from the big sites like YouTube, you have other options as to where you can upload your video. For example, you may be able to find a website that uploads videos and which is designed for your specific market. In the real estate market, there are often websites in which you can post your videos.

Mistakes to avoid with video

Audio and video add novel dimensions and make your site more vibrant and inviting. There are a few mistakes to avoid:

- Don't use audio or video automatically when a visitor arrives at your site. Let people choose to watch video. Otherwise, they will feel that it's being shoved down their throats.

- Don't embed too many videos on one page. This translates into slow load times.

- Seek advice from your website's visitors. If you are considering adding a video, conduct a user survey. If you are already using a video, ask your viewers what they think.

- Video should be an addition, not a subtraction. Don't complicate viewers' lives. Add to them.

Video is popular but still relatively unusual

For the moment, video remains relatively unusual online, with the promise of unlimited creativity. Online video still attracts significant attention. For the moment, a fascination with this medium's relative newness will work in your favour.

In all the video confusion, don't forget the power of the written word

With all the obsession about video, never forget the power of text. Just because people are talking about the power of video does not mean that text is outdated.

The world wide web was created on the power of text and text remains at its core:

- Search engines decide whether or not a page is relevant through text.

- Text is what people use when they seek information.

- Text still remains an integral part of any web page.

- Text should never be replaced by video on your website; text is still preferred by many internet users.

- Text is still extremely easy to transfer and share.

- While text may not have the same dimension or personality as video, it still remains extremely powerful.

- Sales are made through text. Text makes, creates and seals the deal.

The challenge is not to replace text by video. The real challenge is to integrate audio, video and text together in an appealing and powerful manner. Each medium attracts visitors in unique ways. Multimedia boosts your site's popularity as well as your bottom line.

Video boosts the trust factor

The bottom line is that trust is at the core of doing business online. Since a prospect can't see or hear you and in most cases doesn't know who you are, video can help immensely in establishing trust online. With video, your prospects see, hear and touch you, your products and services. Video is both friendly and believable. Video is a valuable tool. Don't squander it.

13 Putting the pieces of the puzzle together

Choosing the pieces of the internet puzzle which are most important for your business

Throughout this book's kaleidoscopic tour, we have examined the pearl-like possibilities available only on the internet. Idea after idea, tool after tool, our businesses can be transformed from good to great. Armed with strategic clarity and authenticity of heart, we can create closer, more dynamic and profitable relationships with customers and employees alike.

Let's look at our Web Wheel (Figure 13.1). On it we see all the topics we have covered: article marketing, websites, search engine optimization, blogs, podcasting, social networking sites, video and viral marketing.

But *now* what do we do? How do we use these tools? Do we use them all? Do we just use a few? Or do we use some now and some later? Which ones should be the priority? How do we decide?

Let's extract the essence of each tool

The best way to get our heads around these tools and understand how we can put them together in the optimal mix is first to review each tool at a time. Let us take each tool and – in one word or phrase –

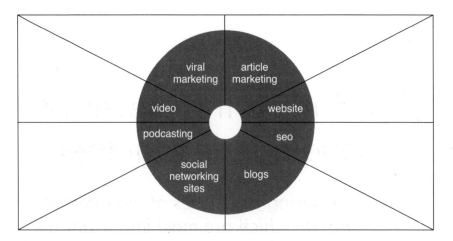

Figure 13.1   The Web Wheel

summarize what that specific tool has to offer. In other words, let's extract the essence of each tool (Figure 13.2).

So, for example, the biggest benefit of article marketing is that it positions you as a thought leader. A website, as the intersection of all you have to offer, will establish your online personality. Search engine optimization will deliver traffic. Blogs help you engage in a conversation. Podcasting speaks to communities of passion. Social networking sites are the pinnacle of interaction. Videos provide high emotion and entertainment. Viral marketing gives you fast exposure.

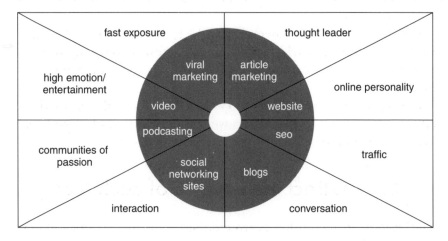

Figure 13.2   Let's understand the essence of each social media tool

Let's look at some case studies

The next step is to try to understand how to use the Web Wheel. By looking at different case studies, we will examine how various combinations of tools on the Web Wheel will deliver the desired response.

In order to discover how this works, we will put together four simple scenarios that will illustrate how the Web Wheel works.

Case study 1

The problem

A small shop in the middle of a wealthy arrondissement in Paris sells premium horseback riding equipment. The shop caters to a high-paying clientele that lives in both the city and rural areas surrounding Paris. While most of the shop's clients are heavy internet users, some have access to high-speed broadband internet connection while others do not. This is a group of people who are passionate about their sport and are willing to pay top dollar for the best equipment.

The shop depends on its small set of loyal clientele but wants to enlarge its base in France and internationally.

Its budget in terms of both time and money is somewhat limited.

The recommendation

My recommendation for this store would be to create the following web programme: create a new website or improve the existing one (establish online personality); offer a weekly podcast (talk to the community of passion); and add some search engine optimization tactics to increase traffic to the site.

- Website creation or improvement:
  - Make it more dynamic and interactive.
  - Offer an e-newsletter and/or white paper. The white paper could talk about a chosen horseback riding subject (eg tips on jumping or dressage), while the newsletter could position the store as an expert on upcoming events and trends in the horseback-riding world. Depending on time, the store may want to consider offering a version for the French market and an English-language version for the rest of the world.

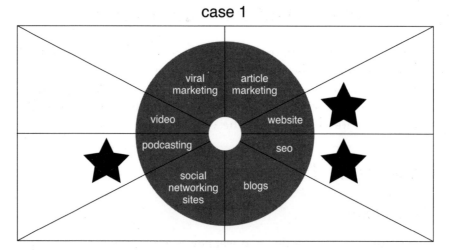

Figure 13.3   Case study one uses three elements of the Web Wheel

- – Create a solid opt-in list so that customers/prospects can be e-mailed regularly.
- Offer a weekly audio podcast (available in both French and English) which speaks to the community of passion (horseback riders).
- Ensure that the site is search engine optimized. Driving traffic to the site through search engine optimization will be essential to growing a broader loyal audience.

Case study 2

The problem

A big US fast-food chain is creating a new product (a vegetarian hamburger that tastes like a regular hamburger). They want to make a big splash across the United States and Europe. However, they don't just want to introduce a product. They also want to connect with customers, prospects and suppliers in another way: showing that they are health-conscious and care about the environment as well as the quality of the food they serve.

Their audience is all ages, but they are particularly interested in attracting a younger audience.

Their budget is substantial but their knowledge about online media is limited.

The recommendation

This company will need to use social networking sites (interaction) and blogs (conversation) in order to help it introduce and discuss some of its ideas about healthy, environmentally friendly eating. In addition, a viral marketing campaign (fast exposure) will be a great vehicle for launching their new vegetarian burger with a big splash. Thus:

case 2

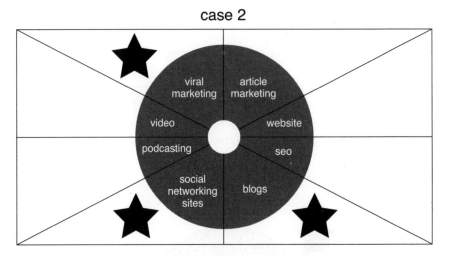

Figure 13.4   Case study two uses three social media tools

- *Blog (conversation).* A blog will help this company begin to have a conversation with key interested parties about products and its new way of thinking.

- *Viral marketing (fast exposure).* With a clever, original video, this company can introduce its new vegetarian burger to potentially millions of people. This is a good vehicle, particularly since it will help introduce a younger audience to its food chain and whole line of products.

- *Social networking site (interaction).* A customized social networking site will allow people to gather around the brand, be entertained as well as learn more about what it means to eat well, even when eating fast food. The company might want to consider introducing a customized widget related to the product introduction.

Case study 3

The problem

A worldwide best-selling author lives in Sweden. He wants to introduce his latest novel as well as get acquainted with his loyal reader base.

The recommendation

This campaign should be launched in two stages.

The first stage would consist of launching a blog (conversation) and creating a profile on a social networking site like Facebook (interaction) to enable the author to have a conversation with his loyal user base.

The second phase of the programme would be to launch a viral campaign distributing a teaser chapter of the book and at the same time releasing a video on YouTube.

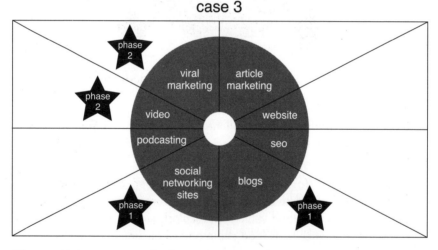

Figure 13.5   Case study three shows how to use social media tools in phases

First phase (social networking and blog)

A blog would be the perfect vehicle for the author to enter into an ongoing conversation with his target audience. He could share all kinds of information about how he writes, what kind of themes he likes or doesn't like and where he finds his inspiration. Readers can discuss this with him and also tell him what books or chapters they like or don't like and why.

A social networking site like Facebook would be a good place to meet new readers as well as talk with loyal readers. The author might want to include some personal details (like what kind of music he likes or his favourite movies), so that he shows his more human side.

Second phase (viral marketing and video)

This viral marketing campaign could be an article or a sample chapter released as a teaser to get readers excited about the forthcoming book release. The author could reward users for spreading the word by offering some kind of discount on the book.

The teaser chapter could be released simultaneously with a video of the author talking about the book or about writing in general. The video should be released on YouTube for maximum viewing.

Case study 4

The problem

A German car manufacturer wants to release its first-ever hybrid car. The company wants to achieve several things with its online programme: introduce its product, establish the company as a thought leader and establish better ties with customers and prospects.

The recommendation

As this company is trying to accomplish a lot, my recommendation here is to roll this programme out in at least two phases. So in the first phase, I would suggest the company start with viral marketing (fast exposure) while simultaneously improving its website (online personality) and its website's readership through SEO (traffic). In this first stage, the company should also launch an article marketing campaign.

The second phase of the programme would include social networking (interaction), a blog (conversation) and podcasting (community of passion).

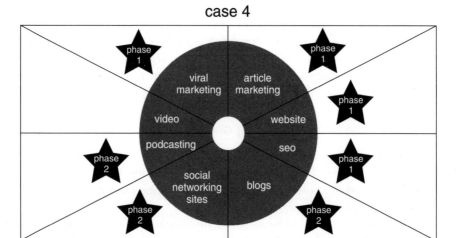

Figure 13.6 Case study four is the most in-depth strategy, using seven tools in two different phases

First phase

The viral marketing programme should probably be in the form of a video. If the company is courageous, it could create a film that doesn't even mention the name of the product until the very end of the video. In any event, the video should not be an advertisement but a unique, quirky piece of communication.

The website would need to be improved, building several pages around the hybrid car buyer and their needs and concerns.

The search engine optimization would need to use keywords around the hybrid car and environmentally friendly products; the company would have to do its homework carefully.

Article marketing would be an excellent means by which to get favourable public relations and establish the company as a thought leader in the area of alternative cars.

Second phase

The company might consider building its own social networking sites around the theme of hybrid cars, building a like-minded community of people around a really important topic.

A blog would be an excellent way of conducting an ongoing conversation with customers and prospects alike and – if the company is feeling brave –

employees would be allowed to contribute to the blog (as in Sun Microsystems).

A bi-weekly podcast on the subject of hybrid cars – what's out there, positive points, negative points, problems, opportunities, etc. This would attract a lot of people, as the subject of being green and environmentally responsible is popular globally.

Figure 13.7 (overleaf) shows all four case studies together and how they compare with one another.

Putting the pieces of the puzzles together is easy if you are clear about what you want to achieve, and understand what each tool brings you. With the Web Wheel, the process is distilled down so you can see clearly what each tool adds to the mix. But in order to use the Web Wheel, you must be crystal-clear about your strategic objectives.

Summary

- Tools are worthless if they are not put together in a sensible and strategic fashion.
- The Web Wheel is an important guide because it distils each internet tool down to its essence.
- You can create a new media programme which has several phases or only one, depending on your needs.
- Confusion reigns on the internet. Be one of the companies that approach the myriad of choices with strategic and tactical clarity.
- To reap what you want from the internet, focus and discipline are essential.

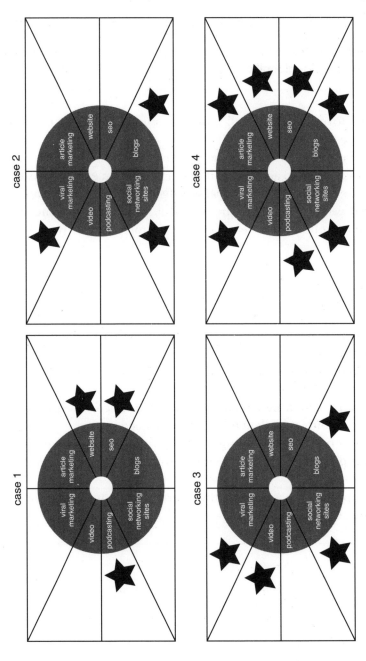

Figure 13.7 Comparing the four Web Wheel case studies

14 A peek at the future

Getting a handle on what is around the corner in the fast-paced, unpredictable world of the internet

This book is a chronicle of tools that already exist and events that have already occurred.

We have toured some of the key newcomers to social media, examining their impact on businesses and people alike.

What have we discovered?

The concept of social media has the potential to overturn traditional media and the concept of communication itself.

Social media corresponds with a larger trend, a trend that is touching us offline and online. That global trend is the fact that people seek comfort in communities and in the human connection they represent.

The age of spin and the mass message is over. People will no longer tolerate them.

It is essential to be authentic.

A two-way dialogue doesn't mean companies have 'lost'. It just means we need to be more focused and disciplined than ever. And that before we as a company act or speak, we must listen.

You need to have a voice that can be heard above the din.

Let your voice have the clarity and calmness that come with reflection.

Listen first. And then you will be heard.

But exciting as all of the above might be, this is just the beginning. What does the future hold?

Social media

Look at how social media will grow. By 2013, it will be several times the size it is today. Once again, the sooner you get on board, the better. You won't want to be a latecomer (see Table 14.1).

But the future is not just about the growth of social media. At many levels, the internet terrain we have reviewed in this book will look like child's play compared to what we will see in 10 years' time. In 50 years, it will be unrecognizable.

Computing power

Computers will change. In 2001, $1,000 worth of computing power equalled one insect brain. In 2023, it will equal the brain of one human being. In 2050, it will equal the brains of all human beings (Figure 14.1). This is almost impossible to imagine.

Table 14.1 Social media should not be ignored; it will get even more powerful in the future

	2007 ($)	2008 ($)	2009 ($)	2010 ($)	2011 ($)	2012 ($)	2013 ($)
Social networking	149	258	437	701	1,063	1,514	1,997
RSS	78	120	182	262	357	463	563
Blogs	64	118	201	290	341	355	340
Wikis	63	108	177	259	342	410	451
Mashups	39	61	98	165	285	458	682
Podcasting	33	50	70	111	158	214	273
Widgets	29	47	75	118	175	250	273
TOTAL	455	762	1,240	1,906	2,721	3,664	4,579

Source: Universal McCann

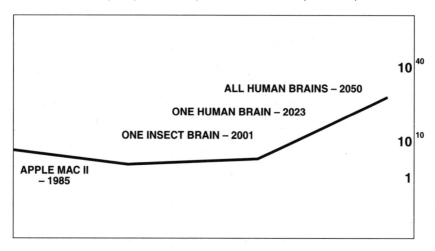

years by which $1,000 of computation equals the intelligence of...

Figure 14.1 The future power of computers makes the mind boggle

Artificial intelligence

Artificial intelligence will enter the scene. In terms of the web, artificial intelligence means intelligent machines.

We have already begun. Amazon introduced aspects of artificial intelligence with Mechanical Turk, their task-management service. It lets computer programs coordinate the use of human intelligence in order to fulfil tasks computers can't do.

The web and artificial intelligence hold great promise. Numenta, a new company created by the tech wizard Jeff Hawkins, attempts to build a new brain-like computing paradigm with neural networks. It hopes to enable computers to tackle human problems like recognizing faces or seeing patterns in music.

Computers compute much faster than humans. The hope is that in the future we will be able to solve problems in ways that we can only dream about today.

Virtual worlds

Virtual worlds are another area that will be developed. Even though Second Life receives lots of mainstream media attention, there are other virtual world opportunities. Virtual worlds will be a vibrant market globally in the next 10 years.

In the future, it will not just be about creating digital lives online. It will also be about making our real lives more digital. So, on the one hand, we will have the rapid rise of Second Life and other virtual worlds. On the other hand, we will begin to annotate our planet with digital information via technologies like Google Earth.

The mobile web

The mobile web is another important new wave. While it is already big in parts of Asia and Europe, it is smaller but growing in the United States.

In 10 years' time, you will be able to get personalized shopping offers through your mobile device as you walk through your local shopping mall. Or map directions through your phone while driving your car. Yahoo! and Google, along with mobile operators, will be key mobile portals.

Many companies – like Nokia, Sony Ericsson, Palm, Blackberry (RIM) and Microsoft – have been active in the mobile web for years. Obviously, the iPhone is another revolutionary step towards the mobile web. The iPhone could easily expand Apple's sphere of influence, from web browsing to social networking and even possibly search. In 10 years' time, the iPhone will probably be seen as the breakthrough mobile web device – at least in the United States.

Personalization

Personalization is another theme. Google was one of the first but there are many others like Last.fm, MyStrands, Yahoo! Home Page and more.

According to Sep Kamvar, Lead Software Engineer for Personalization at Google:

We have various levels of personalization. For those who are signed up for web history, we have the deepest personalization, but even for those who are not signed up for web history, we personalize your results based on what country you are searching from. As we move forward, personalization will continue to be a gradient: the more you share with Google, the more tailored your results will be.

Quoted by Richard MacManus in article published on
ReadWriteWeb.com

Broadband and Wi-Fi

As global broadband grows, the internet will become more vivid, inter-active and emotional. Add Wi-Fi to that and you will have the web everywhere – from your laptop and mobile phone to your PDA.

Online video and internet TV

Online video and internet TV are another trend which will grow expo-nentially. This is a trend which has already exploded but there is a lot more to come. YouTube dominates today. Internet TV services are slowly getting off the ground.

In 10 years' time, internet TV will be totally different. It will have higher quality pictures, more powerful streaming, personalization, sharing and much more (Figure 14.2). The big question is: how will the mainstream TV networks adapt?

The international web

According to the *International Herald Tribune*, by August 2008, China had surpassed the United States as the largest market on the web. This is big news. But there are other countries and regions that are growing by leaps and bounds and that will eventually dwarf the United States' past domination of the web.

For most Web 2.0 applications and websites, the US market makes up over 50 per cent of users. ComScore reported in November 2006

Figure 14.2   Internet TV will be a powerful force

that three-quarters of the traffic to top websites was international. Fourteen of the top 25 US web properties now attract more visitors from outside the United States than from within. That includes Yahoo! sites, Time Warner Network, Microsoft, Google sites and eBay.

It is still early days. In 10 years' time, revenue will be flowing from the international web (Table 14.2). This will be a big change and will

Table 14.2   The international internet carries with it infinite possibilities

World	Population 2008 (M)	Population %	Internet Usage (M)	Population % (penetration)	Usage % of world	Usage growth % 00–08
Africa	955	14	51	5	4	1,030
Asia	3,706	57	529	14	38	363
Europe	800	12	382	48	27	263
Middle East	197	3	42	21	3	1,176
North America	337	5	246	73	18	127
Latin America/ Caribbean	576	9	137	24	10	660
Oceania/ Australia	33	1	19	57	1	154
TOTAL	6,604	100	1,406	21	100	290

Source: Universal McCann

force everyone to rethink how they approach doing business on the web.

The coming digital age holds much promise and great dreams. It will extend human abilities and shrink space. The astonishing variety of the present-day internet with its one billion users is just a small preview of what is to come.

Brace yourself.

References

Anderson, C (2006) *The Long Tail*, Hyperion Books, New York (originally published as article in Wired Magazine, (2004)

Agarwal, A [accessed November 2008] Digital inspiration, the total number of websites on earth [online] http://www.labnol.org/internet/blogging/the-total-number-of-websites-on-earth/2257/

Baker, S and Green, H [accessed May 2008] Beyond blogs [online] http://www.businessweek.com/magazine/content/08_22/b4086044617865.htmB

Baker, S and Green H [accessed February 2008] Social media will change your business [online] http://www.businessweek.com/bwdaily/dnflash/content/feb2008/db20080219_908252.htm

BazaarVoice [accessed November 2008] Online reviewers driven mostly by altruism, CMOs need not fear WOM [online] http://www.marketingcharts.com/interactive/online-reviewers-driven-mostly-by-altruism-cmos-need-not-fear-wom-2527/

Bennett, E [accessed November 2008] The pitfalls, and potential, of social networks [online] http://www.baselinemag.com/c/a/Projects-Enterprise-Planning/The-Pitfalls-and-Potential-of-Corporate-Social-Networks/

Bhargava, R [accessed November 2008] 5 rules of social media optimization [online] http://rohitbhargava.typepad.com/weblog/2006/08/5_rules_of_soci.html

Biddu, S [accessed June 2008] How article marketing can help you gain visibility [online] http://www.selfseo.com/story-19672.php

Business Blog Marketing [accessed November 2008] Business blogs are of vital importance [online] http://www.businessblogmarketing.com/why_blog.php

Cameron-Ruud, J [accessed November 2008] Adopting social media in the enterprise [online] http://www.toprankblog.com/2008/05/social-media-in-the-enterprise/

Caslon Analytics [accessed November 2008] Blog statistics and demographics [online] http://www.caslon.com.au/weblogprofile1.htm#ephemerality

Chan, M [accessed November 2008] Current state of podcasting [podcast] http://cdn.sfgate.com/blogs/sounds/sfgate/chroncast/2006/10/02/TechTalk-20061002.mp3

Cooligan, P and Greene, F [accessed June 2007] The ad is the content and vice versa – profitable podcasting # 9 [podcast] http://www.profitablepod-casting.com/2007/06/28/the-ad-is-the-content-and-vice-versa-profitable-podcasting-9/

Crompton, A (2000) *The Copywriter's Bible* (Mastercraft Series), Rotovision

Dean, K [accessed November 2008] Blogging+video = vlogging [online] http://www.wired.com/entertainment/music/news/2005/07/68171?currentPage=2

Dean, N and McCausey, K (2008) *Easy Article Marketing Attracts Clients, Customers & Partnerships Through Articles*, self-published e-book

eMarketer [accessed November 2008] Social network marketing: ad spending and usage [online] http://www.emarketer.com/Reports/All/Emarketer_2000478.aspx?src=report_head_info_sitesearch

eMarketer [accessed December 2008] Who's watching user-generated video? [online] http://www.emarketer.com/Article.aspx?id=1005856

Everything About Marketing [accessed November 2008] 6 ideas for viral marketing [online] http://marketing-things.blogspot.com/2008/03/6-ideas-for-viral-marketing.html

Graves, L [accessed November 2008] These gizmos connect to the net, but you'd never know it [online] http://www.wired.com/techbiz/it/magazine/16–04/bz_internet

Gunther, M [accessed October 2006] Corporate blogging: Walÿ_Mart's fumbles [online] http://money.cnn.com/2006/10/17/technology/pluggedin_gunther_blog.fortune/index.htm

HighRankings.com [accessed November 2008] What is a title tag? [online] http://www.highrankings.com/allabouttitles

Hill, B (2004) *Building Your Business with Google for Dummies*, Wiley Publishing, Hoboken, New Jersey

Holtz, S and Demopoulos, T (2006) *Blogging for Business, Everything You Need to Know and Why You Should Care*, Kaplan Publishing, Chicago

Huyse, K [accessed November 2008] The 7 habits of highly effective blogs [online] http://overtonecomm.blogspot.com/2006/02/7-habits-of-highly-effective-blogs.html

InternetWorldStats.com [accessed November 2008] Internet usage statistics [online] http://www.internetworldstats.com/stats.htm

iProspect [accessed November 2008] 'iProspect search engine user behavior study' [online] http://www.iprospect.com/about/whitepaper_seuserbehavior_apr06.htm

Jordan, K [accessed December 2008] Definition of search engine optimization [online] http://www.searchenginewiki.com/wiki/SearchEngine Optimization

Kelleher, K [accessed November 2008] MySpace and friends need to make money. And fast [online] http://www.wired.com/techbiz/it/magazine/16–04/bz_socialnetworks

Kennedy Onassis, J (2001) *The Best Loved Poems of Jacqueline Kennedy Onassis* (selected by Caroline Kennedy), Hyperion Books, New York

King, R [accessed November 2008] Building a brand with widgets [online] http://www.businessweek.com/technology/content/feb2008/tc20080303_00 0743.htm

Laycock, J [accessed November 2008] Making link bait and viral marketing work – part eight [online] http://www.searchengineguide.com/jennifer-laycock/making-link-bai-7.php

Layton, J and Brothers, P [accessed November 2008] How MySpace works [online] http://computer.howstuffworks.com/myspace.htm/printable

Learmonth, M [accessed November 2008] Prediction: 40 per cent of video online by 2012 [online] http://www.alleyinsider.com/2007/11/media-exec-survey-40-of-video-online-by-2012.html

Levingston, S [accessed November 2008] Scott Cook quote in Introduction [online] http://www.iht.com/articles/2000/05/24/hype.2.t.php

Levinson, C [accessed December 2008] Asking permission [online] http://www.revenuetoday.com/story/guerrilla-marketing-15

Li, C [accessed November 2008] The future of social networks: social networks will be like air [online] http://blogs.forrester.com/groundswell/2008/03/the-future-of-s.html

Li, C and Bernoff, J (2008) *Groundswell: Winning in a World Transformed by Social Technologies*, Harvard Business School Press, Boston, Massachusetts

Lloyd-Martin, H [accessed November 2008] Copy sells, Flash doesn't: implications for search engine optimization [online] http://www.searchengine writing.com/copysells.html

Macgill Rankin, A [accessed November 2008] Reports: family, friends and community [online] http://www.pewinternet.org/PPF/r/230/report_display.asp

Mack, S and Ratcliffe, M (2007) *Podcasting Bible*, Wiley Publishing, Indianapolis, Indiana

MacManus, R [accessed November 2008] 10 future web trends [online] http://www.readwriteweb.com/archives/10_future_web_trends.php

Maruggi, A [accessed December 2008] Social networking: if you let them build it, they will come: the story of Best Buy's BlueShirt Nation [online] http://www.marketingprofs.com/8/social-networking-best-buy-blueshirt-nation-maruggi.asp

McConnell, B and Huba, J (2007) *Citizen Marketers: When People Are the Message*, Kaplan Publishing, Chicago, Illinois

Meerman Scott, D (2007) *The New Rules of Marketing and PR: How to Use News Releases, Blogs, Podcasting, Viral Marketing and Online Media to Reach Buyers Directly*, John Wiley, Hoboken, New Jersey

Meerman Scott, D [accessed December 2008] The buyer persona blog [online] http://www.webinknow.com/2006/11/index.html

Miliard, M [accessed November 2008] I like to watch; video blogging is ready for its close-up [online] http://www.bostonphoenix.com/boston/news_features/top/features/documents/05145823.asp

Money, R [accessed November 2008] Interview with Rand Fishkin on social media marketing and viral marketing [online] http://www.word tracker.com/academy/rand-fishkin-interview

Moran, M (2007) *Do It Wrong Quickly: How the Web Changes Old Marketing Rules*, IBM Press, Upper Saddle River, New Jersey

Moran, M and Hunt, B (2006) *Search Engine Marketing, Inc. – Driving search traffic to your company's website*, IBM Press, Armonk, New York

Morkes, J and Nielsen, J [accessed December 2008] Concise, scannable, and objective: how to write for the web [online] http://www.useit.com/papers/webwriting/writing.html

Morrison, D [accessed November 2008] Social media: a business marketer's guide [online] http://www.imediaconnection.com/content/14114.asp

Nielsen, J [accessed December 2008] Top ten mistakes of web management [online] http://www.useit.com/alertbox/9706b.html

Noblett, J [accessed March 2008] The corporate blog's dying off [online] http://boston.bizjournals.com/boston/stories/2008/03/17/story3.html?t=pri ntable

Odden, L [accessed November 2008] Entreprise social media – interview with Jim Cuene

Owyang, J [accessed December 2008] What growth in widget networks means to the web strategist [online] http://www.web-strategist.com/blog/index.php?s=using+existing+widgets&sbutt=Go

Parker, S [accessed November 2008] Six article marketing mistakes you must avoid [online] http://ezinearticles.com/?Six-Article-Marketing-Mistakes-You-Must-Avoid&id=938309

Pilot [accessed November 2008] What is article marketing? [online] http://www.articlemarketingautopilot.com/featured/what-is-article-marketing/

Pollei D [online] http://www.toprankblog.com/2008/05/interview-enterprise-social-media/

Revella, A [accessed December 2008] Don't confuse sales support with marketing: a case for buyer persona profiling [online] http://www.pragmat-icmarketing.com/publications/magazine/3/4/0508ar

Ricadela, A [accessed November 2008] What's a widget worth? [online] http://www.businessweek.com/print/technology/content/jan2008/tc200801 7_785524.htm

Rogers, C R [accessed November 2008] Experiences in communication [online] http://www.listeningway.com/rogers2-eng.html from speech given in 1964

Roos, D [accessed December 2008] How social networks work [online] http://communication.howstuffworks.com/how-social-networks-work.html

RSS Applied [accessed November 2008] Search engine visibility via podcasting [online] http://blog.rssapplied.com/public/item/search-engine-visibility-via-podcasting

Rubel, S [accessed November 2008] The hyperconnected vs. 84% of everyone else on earth [online] http://www.micropersuasion.com/2008/05/the-hyper-connec.html

Schefren, R (2007) *From Brick and Mortar to Master Maven*, self-published by Rich Schefren

Sernovitz, A (2006) *Word of Mouth Marketing, How Smart Companies Get People Talking*, Kaplan Publishing, Chicago

Solis, B and Livingston, G (2007) *Now Is Gone: A Primer on New Media for Executives and Entrepreneurs*, Bartleby Press

Spaulding, J (2008) *Article Marketing Domination Version 4*, self-published e-book

Sullivan, D [accessed March 2007] How to use HTML meta tags [online] http://searchenginewatch.com/showPage.html?page=2167931

Sweney, M [accessed November 2008] Ads blow for social networking sites [online] http://www.guardian.co.uk/media/2008/may/21/facebook.myspace

Tapscott, D and Williams, A (2008) *Wikinomics: How Mass Collaboration Changes Everything*, Penguin Group, New York, New York

Thurow, S (2007) *Search Engine Visibility*, Peachpit Press, Indianapolis, Indiana

Veloso, M (2004) *Web Copy That Sells: The Revolutionary Formula for Creating Killer Copy Every Time*, AMACOM, New York

Volvod, L and A [accessed August 2007] Web 2.0 in 5(ish) minutes [online] http://www.epiphaniesinc.com/blog/2007/08/30/web-20-in-5ish-minutes-an-add-info-summit/

Weber, L (2007) *Marketing to the Social Web: How Digital Customer Communities Build Your Business*, John Wiley, Hoboken, New Jersey

Weil, D (2006) *The Corporate Blogging Book: Absolutely Everything You Need to Know to Get It Right*, Penguin Group, New York

Wertime, K and Fenwick, I (2008) *DigiMarketing: The essential guide to new media & digital marketing*, John Wiley, Singapore.

Weston R [accessed December 2008] Social networking strategies for small businesses [online] http://www.forbes.com/2008/03/27/facebook-linkedin-ecard-ent-tech-cx_rw_0327bmightysocialnetwork_print.html

Wikipedia [accessed November 2008] Podcasting [online] http://en.wikipedia.org/wiki/Podcast

Wikipedia [accessed November 2008] Technorati [online] http://en.wikipedia.org/wiki/Technorati

Wikipedia [accessed November 2008] Viral marketing [online] http://en.wikipedia.org/wiki/Viral_marketing

Wikipedia [accessed November 2008] Web 2.0 [online] http://en.wikipedia.org/wiki/Web_2.0

Wilson, Ralph F [accessed November 2008] The six simple principles of viral marketing [online] http://www.wilsonweb.com/wmt5/viral-principles.htm

Winer, D [accessed December 2008] The debate about the worth of podcasting [online] http://www.scripting.com/stories/2008/01/11/theDebateAboutTheWorthOfPo.html

Index